# A Traveler Toward the Dawn

# A Traveler Toward the Dawn

## The Spiritual Journal of John Eagan, S.J.

### Edited by William J. O'Malley, S.J.

A Campion Book

Loyola University Press
Chicago, Illinois

Loyola University Press
3441 North Ashland Avenue
Chicago, Illinois 60657

Library of Congress Cataloging in Publication Data

Eagan, John, 1925—1987.
    A traveler toward the dawn: the spiritual journal of John
Eagan/edited by William J. O'Malley.
    206 p.     cm.
    ISBN  0-8294-0647-6 (pbk.)
    ISBN  0-8294-0706-5 (cloth)
    1. Eagan, John, 1925—1987—Diaries. 2. Catholic Church—
United States—Clergy—Diaries. 3. Jesuits—United States—
Diaries. 4. High school teachers—United States—Diaries.
I. O'Malley, William J. II. Title.
BX4705.E17A3        1990
271'.5302—dc20
[B]                                                      89-48000
                        NA-4879                            CIP

Father John R. Eagan S. J.
1925–1987

# Contents

# Foreword

Helping to prepare the story of my brother's pilgrimage to God has been for me a work of both pain and love.

Of pain, in that it recalled, among a rich store of memories, that last Christmas when John showed me the final chapter of his journal. As I read the powerful image of his house destroyed and rebuilt by God, one of John's favorite books, *I Heard the Owl Call My Name*, leapt to mind. I experienced a distinct premonition that the owl of death was calling John's name. Yet little did I realize that it would be only three short months.

But this task has also been a work of love, because I knew how much this journal meant to John. When Fr. Gene Merz, his 1982 retreat director, suggested to him that he "tell the story of what God has done in you," John's immediate reaction was one of joyful freedom. "What a freeing thing! The whole story bottled up in me, and I had no way to express it. Now at last an avenue is open. I can leave something of myself behind." His purpose was "to put my finger on the Lord's great, faithful love to me—those landmark moments where he touched my life," and "to touch other people's lives by this personal testimony."

Shortly after his death, his former student and devoted friend, Peter Carter, began the laborious typing of John's unrevised, handwritten material. From this rough manuscript, I undertook preliminary editing: deleting repetitions, clarifying meaning, breaking up lengthy paragraphs, and dividing the entire journal into its present chapters and subdivisions. But I felt incapable of the further rigorous editing needed for publication. So I sought an experienced, sensitive editor.

I am enormously grateful to Fr. Bill O'Malley, an accomplished writer, for graciously accepting my request. His expertise and sensitive judgment have brought *A Traveler Toward the Dawn* to its present form.


Joseph Eagan, S.J.
University of San Francisco

# Introduction

Take me to you, imprison me, for I
Except you enthrall me, never shall be free,
Nor ever chaste, except you ravish me.
                              —John Donne

The daily cross in each of our lives is the Big Loneliness. All well and good when routine relieves us of the need to think, when the kids come crying, when the phone shatters the silence, when others' needs give us purpose and meaning. In the midst of that maelstrom, we yearn for quiet, for peace, for being undisturbed. But when the silence and solitude are suddenly there, it is not the gift we really asked for from the wily and whimsical genie in the bottle. Not an oasis, but a void.

One can fill the yawning emptiness with noise. Or busyness. Or autistic enslavement to habit. Or booze. Or one can venture into that great unknown, which seems to our world-wizened eyes a frightening vacuum, a wilderness, unaware that what we believe is nothingness is actually Everything.

Perhaps the metaphor is skewed. It is not venturing at all. It is, instead, waiting, humbly, like a maid in patient, motionless quest of a unicorn. One sits quietly, stripped of all defenses, vulnerable, all the self-inflicted and other-inflicted wounds acknowledged and exposed as a lure to the Healer.

And then he comes, bright-winged and rapacious, aware that he is God. And he enters the soul and possesses what was his from the beginning—all that we had ignorantly and arrogantly believed was ours. "Behold, the handmaid of the Lord. Be it done unto me according to your will." Only thus can Christ be conceived in us.

When John Eagan's brother, Joe, asked me to edit this book, I agreed to read it, condescendingly, as a chore. It was far too long for any publisher to consider, and I had plenty of other busynesses to give my life purpose and meaning. But I began, a reluctant gift to a brother Jesuit and to John, whom I'd known only in passing as a nice, gentle, ordinary priest. No aura, no halo. But as I worked through it with a red pen, cutting whole pages any man or woman would be willing to claim as epitaph, I began to realize I had been invited into the soul of a man privileged to have been ravished by God.

This book is not *The Confessions* or *Seven-Storey Mountain* or *Journal of a Soul*—which makes it all the more valuable. It is the story of God overwhelming a spirit unknown to the wider world, for whom "the manner was ordinary." And thus John makes impregnation by God more accessible to ordinary folk. His book makes it less comforting for us to say, "I'm nobody."

Just as Yahweh chose such unlikely vessels for his light as Noah and Abraham and Sarah, just as the Father chose such unnewsworthy men and women as Mary and Peter and Paul, so God chose John Eagan—who wanted nothing more than to be a good high school teacher.

Ironically, it is rare that God chooses his most beloved from the places we would go looking for them—in the spotlight at center stage. When he circuits the earth, questing, *sicut leo rugiens*, he has so many more "nobodies" to choose from.

To me, the point of John's journal is that we ourselves are the greatest obstacle to our own nobility of soul—which is what sanctity means. We judge ourselves unworthy servants, and that judgment becomes a self-fulfilling prophecy. We deem ourselves too inconsiderable to be used even by a God capable of miracles with no more than mud and spit. And thus our false humility shackles an otherwise omnipotent God.

John Eagan was not such a man.

William J. O'Malley, S.J.
Fordham Prep
Bronx, New York

# 1

## "Dear Friends and Colleagues"

John Eagan died on Passion Sunday, April 12, 1987. Only one month before, on Saturday, March 14, he was told he had terminal cancer. The following Thursday, March 19, he wrote a letter.

March 19, 1987

Dear Friends and Colleagues,

First, let me thank you for your care and concern and prayers, for your notes and flowers and phone calls. This means very much to me.

I'd like to write this letter to you to cue you into what has happened and how I'm feeling about it.

My doctor told me frankly that these cancers are two of the most virulent, that there is no cure for either, with chemo or radiation. The most they can do is delay the process and give me some added weeks or months. But these drugs also have tough side effects.

I asked him how much time I have. He said, I can't say— maybe a year, maybe two, maybe six months. I told them then and there I wasn't interested in chemo and radiation. Just give me as much quality time as I can have. Let me go home and do what I love to do: teach teenagers, for a few more months, do a little travel, visit important people in my life, finish my journal book. And so gently wind up my days and prepare for the final journey to the side of the Lord. My doctors, both men of faith, felt at home with this, promised that they would make me as comfortable as possible, and so released me from the hospital Tuesday, rather than do exploratory surgery.

This may amuse you. Tuesday afternoon I got on my bike and pedaled west for an hour and felt healthy. Wednesday, I taught three classes and rejoiced doing it, though I was very tired at the end. So there's some zip in the old boy yet.

Well, that's the situation. You may ask: how is all this sitting with me now?

Frankly, I'm not depressed. I'm not anxious or afraid. I'm not thinking disaster thoughts or tragedy thoughts. That may come later. Rather, there's a deep calm and peace inside, a gentle yes to the God of my life. I wonder at this, and when I try to analyze it, it comes to something like the following. And I feel at home sharing this with you.

1) I'm sixty-one. I've done most of the things I've wanted to do in life. I've known marvelous people. I've enjoyed priesthood and my work with the young here and out in my fine parish. Life has been good. As I look down the road realistically to my seventies, with diabetes, I'm not enthralled with the possible complications. Rather, in many ways I see it as a real advantage to be told that closure is ahead and soon. First, I feel an enormous sense of relief and a real simplification of life taking place. Second, I feel I have a great opportunity now to prepare for my last and greatest journey, the journey all of us will some day take, to center on the God of my life and to deepen my relationship with him. This getting ready can be a real gift if I utilize it properly.

2) Most mornings of my life I like to get up early, go down to the Blessed Sacrament and put myself in his presence. Once at home with the Lord, I always start my day with Ignatius' little prayer:

"Take, Lord, and receive all I am and have. You've given it all to me; I give it all back to you. Do with me as you want. Just give me your love and your grace and that's enough."

This morning start to each day has, over the years, become the foundation and parameter of my life. So now when the Lord moves in and clearly asks me to travel this way with him, I find that "Yes" to him coming from deep places. And a sense of calm: all's well; I'm in his hands. He'll give me his love and his strength to walk the way till the end.

3) One of the finest things the Society of Jesus has given me is my eight-day retreat. Looking back, I'd say that, since 1981, I've been blessed with landmark retreats. Each has given a stronger and deeper attraction to the very Person of the Lord and a growing desire to be with him. Like a deep pull inside, an undertow. In a way, I feel powerless to describe it, though I'm trying to do it in the journal I have been working on. With the last six years as background then, the cancer thing comes along, and again, here is the Lord of my life moving in on me and telling me "Come home, John. I want you to be with me where I am. I want to share my joy, my love, and risen life with you. It will be grand, and it will be forever." And so deep down I feel myself saying, "Yes, let's go." I want to be with God and basically, I'm as curious as hell about risen life.

Those of you who know me well know that I'm a person who loved to take journeys. So, here I am, at the last and most important journey of my life: to the side of the Lord. Please pray that I may make this last journey in peace, in strong hope of the resurrection, and in growing desire to see face-to-Face this incomprehensible God to whom we give our lives.

Your prayer, your support and encouragement, and your *humor* in the days ahead will mean much to me. Thanks for listening.

John Eagan, S.J.

Please feel free to talk with me about it. I feel very free.

# 2

## Early Years, 1925 - 1971

Avoca, Wisconsin: a sleepy town of 342 people in the Wisconsin River Valley fifty miles west of Madison; a white four-bedroom colonial home at the foot of wooded hills untouched by the Great Glacier. To my father, an accountant graduated from the University of Wisconsin in Madison, and to my mother, a shy, gentle music and art major from the same university, I, John, was born in a snowstorm on November 30, 1925, the second of the three squabbling boys.

Memory fragments: roaming the hills endlessly with my favorite collie, climbing all over Camelhead Rock and the other rock formations that studded the hills, running barefoot in summer grass, biking endlessly, trapping snakes and birds, drifting off to sleep on a summer night with the music of whippoorwills throbbing in my ears, wondering at the wilderness of forest and rock and at the long lines of geese sweeping across the October sky, awakening on Thanksgiving morning to a sudden white world of new snow, thrilling to an exhilarating day of sleigh riding in the hills, coming alive to the world of books with Mr. Rector in seventh grade, returning home after school and my mother at the piano playing Rachmaninoff's piano concerto, enjoying vacations with grandparents in Menominee, Michigan, and sunlit days at beaches, relishing the rhythm of glad family feasts, birthdays, Christmas. Simple small-town joys in the Depression years.

At age thirteen, September 1939, ninety-seven pounds

dripping wet, I was packed off to boarding school at Prairie du Chien, Wisconsin. A whole new life opened up: new friends mostly from Chicago, endless basketball games, systematic study under no-nonsense teachers, jug and strong discipline, walks into the surrounding hills and to the confluence of the Wisconsin and Mississippi Rivers, and a new force, Jesuits.

## Campion Jesuit High School: First Call

It's April of my freshman year. The time has arrived for my first silent retreat. Austy, Jerry, Dick—my Chicago friends—and I gather solemnly in the dorm the day before and pledge to avoid each other for three days and do the retreat in high seriousness. And so we do. On the afternoon of the third day, after much soul searching, I head in for the first general confession of my past life. I wanted to sweep the boards clean. All the young peccadillos, especially three or so I worried about, I had them lined up into a mental list as was the custom then. In a front pew in Our Lady of the Angels chapel, I spoke out my sorrow to God. Carefully I sought out for confessor the oldest, blindest, deafest, and also kindest priest on the faculty, Fr. Ted Schutte, S.J. In the dark confession box with some fear and trembling, I poured out the sins of my fourteen years, hoping he would not recognize me. And then the warm voice of Fr.Schutte, "Now John." He spoke movingly to me of God's great love for me, his mercy, his forgiveness, a mercy that would outlive all my foolishness and malice, and how God wanted me to live a new life and invited me to come close to him. Enormously relieved, I left the confession box and pushed open the door of the church into the beauty of the April afternoon.

How strange. After all these years, I can still relive graphically the sights and sounds and feelings of that blessed moment just as though it happened yesterday. I became acutely aware of the glory of that April day: the pulsing blue sky of early spring, the rich green creeping across the landscape and through the trees, the distant hills standing out clean against the horizon, the ecstasy of awakening nature.

Joy began to well up and run in my heart like an endless river, a joy deep down, rising from some hidden unknown spring, growing and surging in me. And yet a joy qualitatively different from anything I had ever experienced before, purer, richer, unalloyed with anything negative, a full "yes" to all that is. As I walked along, stunned by the newness of it all, that pure, rich joy grew and expanded like a giant dome of air. I don't think I have ever in my life been happier. Over and over through it all, I was so conscious of a new Presence all about me and within me, a Presence I could intuitively name, the great God of the immense universe reaching down into ninety-seven pounds of boy, touching me with his presence in an unmistakably certain way, attracting me strongly, directly, effortlessly to himself.

I wandered along wondering at it all, not knowing or caring where my feet went, my eyes lifted up to the throbbing sky, the soaring swallows, the lush green of spring. At length I found myself way out on the golf course. I remember lying down out of sheer joy on a bunker with my eyes to the blue, blue sky and my arms wide open to the Lord, immensely content, serenely joyful beyond all bounds.

How long I lay there I don't remember. It seemed an hour or so. I felt so close to this God! And then I got up and walked back to the next talk, and life went on.

Strange, though, as I look back. That strong gift of encounter with God in April of my fourteenth year was the landmark beginning of it all. A pure gift sailing in from right field to capture a young lad's heart and to open him to a brand new horizon. I know for certain that my faith was born in that moment, not an abstract faith, but an unshakable certainty that God is real and that I have experienced him. In that hour a deep desire for him started in my depths, an attraction that flames out anew at unexpected times, that runs like a powerful undertow through the years of my life. On that day, the reality of God and his care for me became as clear as the hills surrounding Campion or as the great Mississippi rolling past our doorstep. Over the years, I don't think I've ever been seriously shaken in my faith. For me, faith is simply God's gift, given suddenly at age fourteen in a way that settled me in a certainty not shaken even by later experiences of the suffering of the poor and the human evil that causes it. I marvel at this gift and wonder, "Why me, Lord?"

Stranger still is the aftermath of that first awakening. In the three weeks that followed, it became completely apparent to me, axiomatic, that I was to be a Jesuit and a priest and was to spend my life working with the young. I came to it through no process of reasoning. It seemed a conclusion effortlessly arrived at, with a certainty that left no room for doubt.

I remember sitting in the back seat of the family car on Mother's Day that May at Campion as Dad pushed my senior brother Joe on his college plans. "Son, you've got to decide and let us know. Why can't you get your plans together? What is it that you intend to do?" Finally Joe cleared his throat and told them he had applied to the Jesuit order and would enter in September, and that was that. A shocked silence followed. I'm sure it was the last thing Mom or Dad expected. And I sat in the back seat all ears now, thinking, "So he's decided to go the route I've already decided on."

One night in my senior year I sat down and scribbled off an A-12 scholarship exam for the Army and was surprised to hear I'd won a four-year scholarship to the college of my choice: tuition, books, and living expenses. As I remember, it never really registered on my consciousness as a real possibility. I simply knew where I wanted to go; the matter was settled. So on August 8, 1943, I packed my bags, kissed my parents goodbye, and left little Avoca for the Jesuit novitiate at Florissant, Missouri.

In the years that followed, I've seen many excellent men come and go from this Jesuit order of mine: people far more talented than I, far more gifted in intellect and personality and eloquence. As a Jesuit superior and spiritual director and concerned friend, I've counseled priests and scholastics in time of vocational indecision and tried my best to help them find God's way in peace. I've watched many of these fine men so blessed by God, so beloved by me, leave our ranks. I grieve over this.

Yet for myself I have to say that the central fact of my vocation has always been secure. Even though difficulties pile up, though deep changes forge new crises of adjustment, despite the stark disillusionment that creeps into the midlife "reality" years, the Society of Jesus and the priesthood is the place where God wants me to be. This has never been shaken. This I see as a great gift of God coming to me on a sunny day in April, a gift straight from the loving kindness of this everlasting God. Like some primordial seed in which all later growth is contained, from that first great landmark moment of encounter with God, all else in my life worth having has proceeded and unfolded.

I try to explain this to people, to teenagers on retreat, or to my classes. And all I can do is tell the story of what happened on that April day. Increasingly over the years I wonder at God's gracious generosity stepping into my life, leaving nothing to chance, making it so clear I could not miss it. A constant refrain has been Mary's phrase: "He who is mighty has done great things for me. Holy is his name."

## Jesuit Life

The years now accelerate. New life in the Society of Jesus: the thirty-day retreat in October and the difficult two years of novitiate, a simple, rather austere, regimented life centered on serving Christ. On August 15, 1945, I knelt before the altar with my classmates and vowed perpetual poverty, chastity, and obedience to the Lord. "Take and receive my life." I said "forever" and meant forever. Then two years of classical studies under a superb teacher, Fr. Frank Preuss: the constant joy of reading the ancient greats, Homer and Sophocles, Virgil and Horace; likewise the giants of English literature, Chaucer and Shakespeare, and Milton and Browning, and Wordsworth and Hopkins. Those two years were a joyful immersion in classical art and music and culture.

Then I was sent to Spokane, Washington, for three years of philosophical studies and the companionship of a hundred or so Western Jesuits. For three years I climbed all over the Idaho mountains, summered at a gemlike mountain lake, spent stunning days skiing the slopes of Mt. Spokane, played hockey daily, and made fine new friends at a gracious, friendly Jesuit house on the hill. Our lives were blessed with an outstanding rector, Fr. Bill Elliott, a strong, compassionate man who spoke with inner fire and whom everyone admired and loved. I consider those two, Fr. Preuss and Fr. Elliott, to be the strongest influences and most inspiring role models of my fifteen-year Jesuit training. In a very real sense, they formed me by who they were.

The tempo of life then changed dramatically. I was assigned in 1950 to St. Louis University High School. Green as the hills but excited, I began teaching high school boys English. It was a discovery of the world of teenagers; I led them into literature, coached their freshman football and basketball teams, had endless conversations and informal counseling. All my youthful energy and enthusiasm, pent up by seven years of study, I now poured out lavishly, joyously. I was swamped with work from dawn to dusk, yet I loved it. And young people rallied around me with appreciation and infectious humor.

It's November of 1952, Thursday afternoon. My after-school job is to run the whole athletic operation and care for all the sports equipment and teams. Around 5:30 the last four football teams troop into the basement locker rooms, muddy, tired, but rowdy and exuberant over an impending championship. I'm busy upstairs directing student managers washing jerseys and repairing broken cleats. Suddenly Eddy rushes in shouting, "Mr. Eagan, come quick; the guys are rioting in the locker room." I mutter a fervent, "Oh, damn, that's all I need right now. I'll fix their clock." And so I dash down the long flight of stairs to the riot below.

On a dead run, halfway down the stairs, suddenly I have an acute awareness. An enormous sense of God's presence before me and all around me: the infinite God and myself standing alone in his presence. It was as though I was in a great auditorium alone, and yet a strange auditorium without walls or roof and a sense of infinity in every direction. Ahead of me, on a stage, broad and deep was a radiant center of light streaming toward me, filling my vision. Unmistakably the infinite God. And myself, tiny before him, yet standing straight and walking towards that light with a profound sense of awe and wonder. God was a warm and benevolent and attracting presence, yet somehow infinite and transcendent at the same time. It was a sudden taste of another world in this most unlikely of all grubby moments.

This was, as I remember it clearly, just a split-second of acute awareness as I raced down the stairs, filled with Irish impatience, determined to stamp out insurrection below. And then it was gone.

I turned the corner, rushed into the locker room, eyes blazing: "Cut the crap; get your equipment out; get into the shower; ten minutes and you're all out of here, or it's Saturday jug for the lot of you. Why don't you grow up?" Muttering unprintable things, I returned to the upstairs cage, finished my work, locked up, and went over to the Jesuit community for a late dinner. The current of a very busy life went on. But later in the days ahead I wondered at this unique moment, strangely apart from all other moments. How unexpected! As the weeks lengthened into months and the months into years, that split-second moment of vision loomed larger and larger in my consciousness. So many important incidents and memorable moments in those busy happy years have faded from my memory. But this simple moment stands out now in stark relief like some huge desert pyramid or Easter Island figure. The moment when God again suddenly intervened in my conscious life and declared himself in a way I can never forget. Infinity, "from everlasting to everlasting you are God"; light, transcendence, and myself, small, utterly alone before him, taken from the multitude and standing in all my littleness and uniqueness before him, yet this great God inviting me.

I cannot assign any reason for this, any preceding cause. I cannot say what it effected in me. It simply stands there as another landmark moment of those thirteen years of Jesuit training. I still wonder at it.

## Ordination and Priesthood

In 1953 came the difficult transition from the teaching years I so dearly loved to studying again; it was a dreadfully un-

happy year of theology studies out in the remote Kansas hinter-
land. But then came satisfying second and third years as
priesthood drew near. A joyful eight-day retreat before ordination given by everybody's favorite old mystic, Fr. Dannegger
("the Beatific Vision, don't I know!") and then quickly ordination in Milwaukee, June 20, 1956. The powers of priestly ordination spill over me as I kneel before the bishop, bewildered by
the suddenness and depth of it all; then the first priestly
blessing to my father and mother, my brothers, my former St.
Louis High students. And one breathtaking moment early the
next morning when, before a small group of family and students, I opened the missal for my first solo Eucharist and read
the entrance hymn, "What is man that you should think of him,
the son of man that you should care for him? You have made
him a little less than the angels, with glory and praise you have
crowned him."

The whole wonder of my priesthood suddenly registered.
Here I am in my thirty-first year, called from a little town in the
hills of southwestern Wisconsin, rich with God's graces, standing at the altar to celebrate my first Eucharist. How enormous
is God's goodness to me. A tide of wonder and gratitude welled
up in me. I could not speak. Then, slowly, in a trembling voice
I spoke the words, "I will go to the altar of God, to God who
gives joy to my youth."

Then swiftly the final two years of Jesuit training. Some
special priestly moments: hearing my first confessions during
a thunder and lightning storm and the sincerity of the people I
brought Christ's forgiveness to that day; two action-packed
weeks as chaplain at St. Francis Hospital in Topeka, immersed
in the needs of the suffering and the dying; a joyous working
with Indian teenagers from all over the United States at Haskell
Indian Institute in Lawrence, Kansas, during my final year of
theology studies; then to cap my formation as a Jesuit a final
year of spiritual training in Decatur, Illinois, featuring the
thirty-day retreat experience of the Ignatian Exercises again;
and during that Lent seven straight weekend retreats for lay-
men at the Jesuit Retreat house outside St. Paul, a work that I
loved.

When superiors offered me Ph.D. studies, first in English,

then psychology, my determined response was: "What I would really love to do is return to a Jesuit high school as fast as I can and spend my years teaching my favorite crowd, teenagers."

## Marquette High School

And so the call to teach at Marquette University High School in Milwaukee. I settled into my new home in August of 1958, itching to begin. I lavishly poured out my enthusiasm, so long pent up, and I loved the hard work and the long hours: nine closed retreats each year; Sodality or Christian Life Community programs for kids who wanted more of Christ and spirituality; non-stop counseling; sharing with senior classes my love of Chaucer and *Macbeth* and *Hamlet* and Browning and Wordsworth and Hopkins and T.S. Eliot; city-wide Sodality union work with a yearly sodality leadership workshop; summer camping trips in Ontario: all this backed by a Jesuit community well-known for its warmth and friendliness and good times together. Then five summers of jetting all over the United States with the SSCA (Summer School of Catholic Action), a traveling troop of priests and lay people giving week-long courses on the full Christian life in major U.S. cities. This made possible side trips into favorite spots like Yosemite and Mt. Rainier, the Olympic Peninsula and the Big Sur and Padre Island, and always the Pacific Ocean. The years passed in a blur of enthusiastic work, the joy of those early years of priesthood.

A sudden wrench. My mother at sixty-eight is felled by a stroke. We arrive at her side, comfort her; two days later a final stroke takes this gentle woman, the affective heart of our family, a presence I had always counted on. Raw, primeval grief swept over me, surprising me by its depth and intensity. It was as though a giant tree had been pulled, roots and all, out of my soil. Mom's death left an aching hole behind. And yet on November 1, 1965, All Saints Day, somehow we managed the Mass of Christian Burial and joy broke through. A good woman gone home to God. Yet in my fortieth year of life, for the first time, intimations of mortality break in.

Nineteen sixty-five brought the challenges of Vatican II

and the excitement of renewal. I plunged in, determined to drink deeply of the "new" scripture and the "new" theology. I hit the best: brilliant Ray Brown and Bernard Häring at the University of San Francisco, Barney Cooke and John Sheets and Quentin Quesnell at Marquette, Avery Dulles and Gregory Baum and Barnabas Ahern at the Maryknoll Summer School. Scripture, grace, morality, church were the areas of choice for my renewal work for five summers. In my teaching I shifted gears to teach a marvelous group of freshmen the Old and New Testaments; for years I enjoyed rooting myself anew in the great biblical themes.

A sidelight. Ever since 1963 I've chosen to take my summer vacations by organizing camping trips with groups of teenagers who love nature and long to get away from the noise of cities into pure wilderness. Our choice has always been the Lake Superior country: the Porcupine mountains, Pictured Rocks, Lake Superior Provincial Park. Here veined Pre-Cambrian rocks, the world's oldest at 3.5 billion years, dive precipitously into the loveliest and wildest of our Great Lakes, a lake so pure you can stand in it and drink. We would set up camp at Coldwater, far from people, hike all over the granite headlands and back up along the rivers that fall some 400 feet on their way to the lake, dive into the holes below the waterfalls, and then settle down at sunset for memorable Eucharists that touched us all so deeply. We would close out the evening with an hour or two of stunning star-show or the sudden gift of occasional northern lights fascinating us to awed silence, then a bonfire and a teeth-rattling midnight swim in cold Lake Superior. Sometimes I wonder if these days so filled with fun aren't the best work I do for young people.

## Bill Peiffer

In August, 1971, I was set once again for a two-week camping trip with five seniors in a class I'm very close to. The day before the trip, Bob Seelman called in with a bad case of poison ivy, "Sorry, I can't go." I thought of Bill Peiffer, a senior, a cross-country runner, a member of my CLC group working with juvenile offenders at the county home. I caught Bill as he came in from his last day at work. Yes, he was free; yes, he wanted to go. He scurried down to pick up my dittoed list of details, went home and packed, and so joined us. For two weeks we reveled in that Lake Superior world. The Coldwater campsight was as untouched as ever; we marveled at the great veined rocks that ran like tongues out into the lake and sparkled in the clean sunlight. We hiked the Sand and Baldhead Rivers, swam their current; dived in holes boiling with foam below their waterfalls. Each night Bill joined us in a Eucharist the lads had planned themselves. After taking Communion, each would go off to a favorite spot for twenty minutes of prayer with the Lord, returning for shared prayer and the final blessing.

Bill entered into the outdoor stuff fully; he was a strong hardy kid with reserves of energy built by cross-country conditioning. Three times without apparent fatigue, he climbed straight up the Devil's Slide, a five-hundred-foot sand dune near Grand Marais. But I did notice an unusual thing: whenever we crossed streams bridged over by fallen trees, Bill always went down on all fours and proceeded cautiously. I kidded him about this. On the second-to-last day of the trip, Bill was sitting quietly on the shore while the rest of us where playing water football. When I asked him what was wrong, he told me he had a bad headache. I gave him an aspirin and forgot it.

On his return, Bill went out for cross-country and began training. But to his frustration, this healthy young man began tripping over his own feet. Then he began to notice that along with his headaches came shooting rays of light, sunstarts in his eyes. Alarmed, he went to his eye doctor, a good friend of mine, who advised him to have it checked by a brain specialist. His mother, Frances, watched the symptoms mount with horror. She had seen her husband die of a brain tumor six years before. Bill was all she had. The day of the operation another priest and I sat with Frances for the seven-and-a-half hour operation. At the end of that long day, the brain surgeon told us he had removed a malignancy the size of a potato behind Bill's ear but that the cancer had gone down into the brain stem and so he could not get it all. A death warrant. We talked with Frances. And then I went into the recovery room and watched this healthy lad, Bill, struggling for life, his head bound in white.

But he rallied, came to, and spoke to us. From early September till early November, with sheer guts and pluck he hung in there. But he never left the hospital. Our kids, his fellow seniors, flocked to his bedside to be with him and with his mother. After school, after football practice, after Senior Follies practice, night after night they came; and a core of close friends, some eight or ten, remained each night till Frances went home. Then they went home and started their homework, often finishing after midnight.

Bill slipped in October as the cancer wrenched life from him. I'll never forget one night in mid-October. I was rushing out to a ski sale when the call from the hospital came, "Come over fast. Bill just stopped breathing." When I got there, Bill was breathing again and the crisis was over. I walked into the sixth-floor waiting room; the kids were deathly quiet; Frances sat there, knuckles white as she grasped the arms of the chair. Luckily, I did it right. I took her out to the darkened chapel where we knelt and prayed side by side for twenty minutes. You could almost feel the strength returning to her. Finally, she turned and said with a smile, "I'm ready. Let's go back. Those kids need us. Thank God, Father, we have faith and the Lord and his strength. Without that, where would we be?" And I saw her move back into that room with a smile and speak to each senior and cheer them up and send them home. I marveled at this strong woman.

Bill died in early November. One night when he was in a coma and it was obvious he was slipping away, sixty or seventy Marquette High School students gathered in a packed reception room on the sixth floor. There Don Driscoll and I celebrated a Mass centering on Paul's psalm on resurrection and the 15th chapter of Corinthians and John's Last Supper promise of everlasting life. It was a time of coming to grips with the reality of death and the radiant promise of Jesus' resurrection for us all, but especially for these lads and their girl friends. We invited the kids to speak; I'll never forget that night. One after another those young people spoke, slowly, intensely, of their own gropings for meaning in the face of death, of their own faith, of what life was all about for them, of hope and resurrection, and

Bill, and themselves. Then we gave them the Food that is a sure pledge of risen life.

Several days later I celebrated the Mass of Christian Burial at St. Rita's, Bill's home parish. The church was packed with family and friends and with hundreds of our Marquette High kids. Then we buried young Bill. May the angels and saints welcome you to paradise, Bill.

## Rector of Jesuit Community

Back to 1968. Suddenly my life took the most unexpected of turns. Our new principal and I were summoned in November to a late-night meeting with Fr. Joe Sheehan, our Wisconsin provincial, head man of the Jesuits for our seven-state area. There he informed us that our president-rector had been assigned a new mission in Argentina. Our principal had been invited to be the president of the school; I was asked seriously to consider the job of rector of the Jesuit community: forty men ranging in age from 25 to 85. I walked back to my room that night stunned. The words of Fr. Sheehan stuck in my mind, "Sometimes God calls a person and opens a new way." That night I lay in bed and let my mind rove for hours. Surprisingly it dwelt mostly on all the good things that needed to be done for the fine men I lived and worked with. I saw it as an opportunity to serve and to give warmth and encouragement and personal care. The next morning I called in my yes.

This was a fateful decision that enormously complicated what had been up to now a simple, straightforward, serene, happy time serving the Lord's young people. Little did I realize that I was being promoted beyond my competence, into very troubled waters indeed. My three-year stint as rector coincided with what some people felicitously remember as the "glory years," 1968 to 1971, when everything in American society and in religious life was held up for the most radical kind of questioning and dramatic change. Jesuits, from priests to scholastics, left in droves. And here was John Eagan, in all his naivete, bright-eyed and optimistic as ever, grappling with one of the most baffling periods of change in the Jesuit order. A baptism by fire. On entering the job, I was informed immediately that one of my priests, a good friend, would leave the Society and priesthood and marry, and I was to handle the details. Within two weeks one of our teaching scholastics headed over the hill for Texas without a word of explanation and was never seen again. Then a young Jesuit brother went East and out of the order. Welcome, John, to the territory.

But the new job did go well. We installed a more collegial style of governing, were careful to elicit the advice of all in the house on every new course of action, and we tried to foster co-responsibility and a warm, friendly spirit. The house minister's job (care of all the physical details; cars, food, heating, supplies, etc.) was split into twenty segments and farmed out to different community members so that all were responsible for all. Hospitality to visitors was a high priority of mine; our house became known for its friendliness and easy humor. For the first time in sixteen years, together we decided to renovate our institutional style of residence. A hot debate ensued over poverty, but rugs and new furniture transformed our rec rooms. Dark wood paneling covered over the green hospital tile in our dining room and provided a warm pleasant dining area. Wall murals and racing stripes brightened our halls. Much of the work we did ourselves, and for a modest sum, thanks to our loyal alumni. I started a special academy that met monthly before dinner, one month featuring a well-known theologian speaking on some facet of renewal in theology, the alternate month bringing in a speaker on spirituality and prayer.

But in the rush of my enthusiasm, I attempted too much. Foolishly I wound up somehow each year with a regular class-load of four theology classes daily, took all eighty-five kids who signed up for counseling with me, ran two youth CLC groups and one excellent married couples group, and gave four CLC retreats a year. All this while supervising the details of a busy community's life and being available in an unlimited way to the beck and call of any Jesuit in need of pastoral care. Eventually, after two years, the job took its toll and chronic fatigue began to settle on me.

What really did me in, however, were the crisis situations

I kept running into, the people problems. The human drama of fine men called by God to serve and yet wrestling with their demons and desperate moments of suffering. For instance, after working with a fine young priest in whom alcoholism was becoming painfully, publicly clear, even scandalous, there came the moment when I had to intervene (this with no background, no training) and ship him off to Guest House for months of treatment. Yet it did not work: five years later he would die by his own hands, hanging, in South Dakota. Suicide was always a bottom-line possibility with him, and I knew it. Another fine teacher would go on wide manic-depressive swings each year, lashing out with imprudent, hostile behavior and then lapsing into the grimmest of depressions for months at a time. Nothing would help.

For the first time in my life, I found myself running into doorless walls, no solution in sight anywhere, damned if you do, damned if you don't. By Easter I was unable to sleep before three in the morning and stared night after night at the ceiling waiting for healing sleep. Exhausted, I dragged myself over to Campion for an eight-day retreat and so limped into summer reprieve. But I could not bounce back. It slowly became obvious to me that, in taking this job, I had badly wrenched the current of my life out of its basic course. I tried once more, but by Thanksgiving of 1971, it was obvious that I was burned out, fatigued beyond measure, and that any further steps along this path would prove ruinous to my health and perhaps injurious to my community. In short, I asked to be relieved of this rectorship and to be allowed to return to my first love, teaching youth. And so it was granted.

Sadder, soberer, yet wiser, I began to sing my "Born Free" and returned to the simple life of a teacher.

Little did I know how, at age forty-six, everything in my life was about to change.

**3**

---

# A Second Beginning, 1972 - 1973

## Tomb of John XXIII: The Second Call

It's now June 8, 1972. My seventy-nine-year-old father and I are in Rome visiting my Jesuit brother, Joe, who is in the midst of doctoral studies in ecumenical theology at the Gregorian University. We've put in three full days of sightseeing, marveling at standard tourist spots such as the Forum, Colosseum, the lovely fountains of Trevi and Navone, the Sistine Chapel, and the great basilicas. The morning finds us in hard-won first-row seats at Pope Paul VI's weekly audience. Six thousand pilgrims from all over the world cheer wildly as the Pontiff is borne in on the sedia. I nod through his forty-five-minute speech in Italian. Then, to my great surprise, Paul comes down and shakes hands with each of us in that front row, turning back at my brother's bidding to embrace my father when Joe tells him Dad is the father of two Jesuit priests. Certainly the high point of Dad's Rome trip. This moment the ever-present photographers catch in color.

After lunch and a short snooze, I set out solo on a walk to St. Peter's in Vatican City to explore it my own way. I wander through the spacious square past the great fountains, through Bernini's columns and into the basilica. I stare at the markings in the floor depicting graphically how Westminster and other great churches of the world are dwarfed by this, the largest of churches. Then section by section I tour the body of the basilica, growing vaguely distressed by eighteen-foot heroic statues of popes and founders of religious orders lunging out at me. I stand in front of Bernini's baldacchino over the main altar and stare at the giant sunburst over the papal chair. I'm tired; jet lag plus three days of sightseeing have taken their toll. And I'm a bit depressed and annoyed by the lavish interior of St. Peter's and the glorification of the papacy. I wonder, "What does this all have to do with the humble carpenter of Nazareth? Would he be at home with this rampant triumphalism?"

Then I wander into the dark basement and blunder into the altar and tomb of Pius XII, the saintly pope of my boyhood. There I kneel and pray a while. It's almost like meeting an old friend. Tired and somewhat down, I turn a corner and am greeted by a flood of light, a cream-colored tomb with some wilted flowers and a few candles burning; twenty or so people are kneeling in prayer. Chiseled on the front of the tomb, the simple words: Pope John XXIII.

Suddenly, without warning I felt within me an incredible pull coming from that tomb as though an invisible force were attracting me with irresistible strength. Enormous desire for the living God flamed out in me. I felt as though my heart were being pulled out of my very body. I was overcome by a great longing for the loving God, to be a good priest, to be at last a man of God, one whose whole life was centered fully and finally on him. It seemed so very clear to me at that moment that an old way of living had come to an end and a whole new way had been opened up for me. The clear image in my head was that of turning over chapters of a book and being finished with them for good and opening the book to a brand new chapter on which nothing had yet been written. I had a clear intuitive sense that this was a landmark moment in my life, a watershed event, that my future life would be dated from this moment, that all else in my life till then was just a prelude. This entire event stunned me by its suddenness, its intensity and depth, its sense of certainty.

How long I lingered there and savored that moment, that overwhelming desire for God, that surge in me wanting to be completely centered on him, I can't remember. But I remember stumbling out of the dark basement into the bright sunlight of

the piazza, dazed at what had happened, unable to comprehend it or put it into any perspective. How impoverished
human words are to capture such experiences!

This unexpected grace cascading over me as I meandered
through St. Peter's, tired, cynical, and somewhat depressed, on
June 8, 1972, was simply once again God moving directly into
my life, unmistakably encountering me, summoning me to
himself, opening up a brand new, qualitatively different chapter in my life. Effortlessly, in a way that defies description, the
whole landscape of my life is altered and reorganized. Age
fourteen, age forty-six, the decisive moments of my life as I see
it now, the times when great new currents were cut loose in my
life by this God who loves me.

That day at John's tomb opens up a poignant question: how
does a person in a limited, imperfect, human life answer a call
to total self-giving? How do I do this in any effective sense? For
years I have wrestled with this. The call is so clear, so unmistakable, so deeply moving, so often repeated, especially in my
eight-day retreats since that day. But the question persists: how
does one in day-to-day living respond with anything approach-
ing totality?

Yes, it seems a brand new chapter has begun. It is bewildering as I stumble into this future. Lord, what are you doing so
suddenly in my mid-forties? Where are you going? What is
this?

Confronting the infinite God of love who invites you in the
middle of life is a humbling experience.


### Fr. Marty Palmer

After jetting home from Rome, with scarcely enough time
to do my laundry and sleep off jet lag, I journey to Campion for
a two-week intensive summer religious education institute for
seventy Jesuit high school theology teachers. Awaiting us as
our scripture teacher for a week is a new person in my life, the
gentle, modest, brilliant Fr. Marty Palmer. Marty chooses for
our consideration one of the great currents of scripture: Jesus,

the supreme revelation of the Father. The insights I gain this week become central categories for my future thinking and teaching and preaching. Marty moved in the following vein:

God in Himself is the transcendental one. As such he exceeds and explodes all our human thought categories. No human mind can capture Him. He who is light in himself is darkness for the human mind.

How, then, can he communicate himself to fleshbound human beings in a way calculated to grasp us and grip us and lift us up into a lifegiving personal relationship with him?

The first way God chooses to bridge the gap is creation. He creates our universe, the bewildering variety of touchable, seeable, hearable, palpable beings, so that we can stand before star-studded heavens, before sunrise and sunset glories, before Yosemite and Coldwater, the might of the Pacific in storm, before the complexity of atom and DNA and the human body, and know something of that Maker: his majesty, his intelligence, his beauty, his power. In a real sense, "the world is charged with the grandeur of God." Creation is the first preaching of the good news. The universe is truly a sacramental universe, a sign disclosing Him. He is the radical secret at the heart of the universe. And so it has been for me in my experience.

But he chooses to bridge the gap in a more significant, personal way. He chooses out of many nations one people and in the years of their history discloses—progressively from Abraham and Moses on, but most specifically in Isaiah and Jeremiah and Ezekiel and Hosea—his holiness, his desire for human beings, his longstanding, faithful love for his rational creatures.

And yet this is not enough. He must say it in a way no one can miss. He must lay his heart open to us and give us the supreme argument of love. He must pour out his inmost identity in an ultimate symbol worthy of himself which would convince us even in our cynicism.

Thus, the final way he gladly chose to reveal himself is in his own Son, existing before the stars, who would become a limited human being with a body like me, an emotional life like mine, a thinking loving spirit, and a developing identity—consciousness like mine. So Jesus begins life as an infant and grows up in a backwater town, takes up the carpentry trade, is called at the Jordan ford and teaches and heals and forms a small group of followers, dies and rises. And precisely through this short life of carpenter and teacher, God the Father is revealed to the world in stunning clarity. Jesus then is the great sacrament, symbol, revelation of the very depths of the incomprehensible God. What Jesus reveals is the Father's love for us humans: a self-giving love unto death, an unconditional love accepting our flawed condition, forgiving endlessly our weakness and malice.

Yes, all this is revealed, perhaps best in the Gospel of John, chapters 13 - 17. God's crowning revelation is not, however, through Jesus' strength, his miraculous power, his awesome qualities, but precisely and paradoxically through his very weakness, his anguish and tears, through his cry of desperation on the cross. We see a peasant trapped by religious authorities, pushed and shoved from one tribunal to another through a sham trial, beaten like a dog, crowned with insults, led like a bleeding animal to the Calvary rock, nailed to beams, stretched out against the sky naked, and dying like an animal. This he would do for me. In his agony he reveals to me who God is and how much God cares, this in a way I can never forget. "Whoever sees me, sees my Father." "And I, if I be lifted up, will draw all to myself." The *kenosis*, the emptying of self till nothing is left to give. Now I know in the flesh of Christ, in his agony of spirit how much this God loves me and seeks me and wants my intimacy. To come to realize this is salvation already begun, eternal life already started in time. To say yes to this love and to welcome him and his Father and his Spirit is the heart of any life.

I returned to Milwaukee conscious of a great and unexpected gift.


## An October Night at Door County

October, 1972. Once again we survive the annual rush of launching another school year. Four of us Jesuit priests head for a weekend of vacationing and sightseeing in Door County, a thumblike peninsula jutting up into Lake Michigan. It's colo-rama weekend; the maples are in full flame. All day Saturday we hike lovely Peninsula Park, tour through the picturesque towns of Fish Creek, Ephraim and Sister Bay, climb around the limestone cliffs at Cave Point, enjoy a flaming fish broil. Around 11:00 we tire and so meander off to sleeping bags. But I put on a sweater and ski jacket and set out to do a favorite thing, walk the long stretch of beach.

It's a cool October night, the darkness lit only by starlight, a strong wind blowing in from the east, whitecaps streaming shoreward as far as the eye can see. The evening is filled with the sound of surf. From the moment I move out onto the beach, I experience a sudden, vivid sense of the Lord's presence filling the night all about me in the glory of nature and in the depths of my heart. My spirit quickens and swings out to the Lord and begins to soar like a jubilant gull riding the buoyant currents. Joy and peace stream into me as my soul expands in the bracing night wind. For an hour or so I walk that beach as close to the waves as I dare, filled with this clear sense of God all about me and within me. The infinite God of the vast universe, of starlight and cosmic space reaching down from infinity to touch my life on this October night. "O, taste and see that the Lord is sweet." "From everlasting to everlasting you are God." It's so easy to pray now, but prayer seems beyond words. Rather, it's a deep longing for this living God welling up within me like a spring. I become acutely aware of the strong wind blowing in from the east and of the crashing waves. The wind, breath of the night, great symbol of the Holy Spirit, Jesus' last gift to us. A profound sense of the Spirit settles over me, the Spirit of Genesis blowing across the chaos of first creation, the mighty wind that rocked Pentecost house. My prayer settles on one desire, one only, "Come Holy Spirit, come, fill my life." It was an effortless mantra rising from my very core, meeting the God of wind and sky.

I return, unroll my sleeping bag, and lie there in silence. I marvel again at this God who moves with such masterful freedom when and where he wishes, the God of surprises who comes to claim human hearts.

## First Directed Retreat

Early June, 1973. With some trepidation I approach my first directed retreat at the Jesuit Retreat House on the shores of Lake Winnebago near Oshkosh. The director I've asked for is Fr. Peter LeBlanc from Guelph, Canada, a Jesuit my own age. I wonder what this personally-directed retreat will be like.

In February I was felled by a stubborn virus that put me on my back for a week. For a month I couldn't recover my energy. I began teaching again and then fell apart and had to rest. So I followed a deep bent, made the best out of a bad situation, and went on a reading tangent that led me through some eighteen books in a week. Bernard Bassett's book *Let's Try Praying* was my starting point. That led me to four other books Bassett suggested and ultimately to some of the best charismatic literature. David Wilkerson's classic *The Cross and The Switchblade*, a book that triggered the Catholic Charismatic movement at Duquesne University, was a discovery.

I've always loved to read. Thank God, I read fast. I love to go hitch-hiking in books whenever I get a chance, to let one book lead me to another and that to another until a journey has been taken, one with a definite beginning, a middle, and an end. I've gradually come to see that my reading is a key to who I am and where in life I'm going. It's a great cue as long as I stick with what is white hot in me and what evokes deep resonance. During that sick spell I was surprised to find myself centering on the Holy Spirit and the work of the Spirit in the lives of real people today.

Another blow in May. A phone call from Denver and I learned that one of my closest friends in the Jesuits, Fr. Ed Maguire, had just died of a heart attack. This grand man, affectionately dubbed "Moose," an all-city football and basketball player at Regis, is gone. For years we had traded elbows on the basketball court and had endless highly competitive games of Indian ball. This Moose had a heart as wide as all the earth. Shortly after his death, a Jesuit from New Orleans called me and said, "This was the kindliest man I've ever known. I've never, not even once, heard him cut anyone down." And he was right. Ed was always the defender of the underdog, champion of the defenseless, one who would terminate a humorous cut-down session with a strong statement on the goodness of the man under fire. I loved this big-hearted man who gave so much of himself to his Jesuit brothers, to the high school kids who mourned him and dedicated a fieldhouse in his honor. A giant loss. A redwood missing from my horizon.

Yes, these things were on my mind as I entered this retreat. Plus a gentle sadness at the aging process going on in me: the loss of more teeth, the slow diminution of energy and health that often marks the forties. I'm finding that a number of things that once exhilarated me and were great fun were slowly coming to an end and turning into dust. I had a gut feeling that began to emerge to consciousness that my life as a Jesuit teacher was words, words, words, a whole blizzard of them, and those words felt increasingly empty. The deeper bent in me, struck open by life, yawned on.

In the first talk with my director, Peter, I decided to open myself as totally as I could. So I explained all that had been going on in my life, especially since 1968 when the superiorship fell on me. I told him that I felt like an old battered car that had been hit from every side: fenders crunched, front and rear bashed in, and yet still able to limp along life's highway. Peter listened carefully and then told me just one thing: "John, as Israel in the Old Testament was so fond of doing, going over again and again their history and recounting the mighty acts of their God, so in the days ahead I want you to take a searching look at your own life story." He advised me to focus on my own personal history, God's gracious interventions in my life, the way he has worked in me and in the concrete events of my life over the years to bring me where I am today. I was to recount the acts of God in my life and to see the whole as my own salvation history.

The simplicity of all this! A grand theme that united all the diverse things that had been stumbling around dumbly inside me awaiting insight and expression. When he advised this, it was as though scales fell from my eyes.

I left Peter's room around 9:30 that night filled with this overriding insight, and I went for a long walk along the lake shore. From the moment I stepped out into the fresh night air, the whole night seemed alive with the Lord, living and moving in his creation: the strong breeze from the north, the low clouds scudding overhead, the waves crashing in on the rocks, the clouds of lake flies singing in the trees, the nesting birds calling out in the night, the large night bird that swooped down on me with a wild raucous cry whenever I approached his turf. It seemed then that all of creation around me was singing out joyously to God that spring night and thrilling in ecstasy. My every sense and whole being resonated with that ecstasy.

Then the overarching thought came through: this great God of nature, this creator of stars and lake and wind, this Spirit of life that animates all that lives and breathes and moves, this very same God was continuously bending tenderly to me and filling my emptiness and my battered poverty of spirit with his fullness; he was working in my life history with care and purpose and strength and drawing me, 180 pounds of dust fading into middle age, event by event, experience by experience, into himself: the Center. Yes, there is a story in me and it is going somewhere. The Potter is forging his piece of pottery out of my poor clay. The Master Tapestry-Maker is weaving his own tapestry out of the stuff of my life. The Good Shepherd is leading me on a journey to rich gracious, green pastures.

I was stunned by the sense of God all about me and within me. I was overwhelmed at his gracious love for me in the fabric of my life. For an hour and more I walked on, caught up in this God. Prayer was no effort. It was simply being with him listening and seeing and being filled with him and speaking words that welled up from my depths. It was like putting my finger on the ecstatic pulse of the world. In the wonder of it all, I tumbled finally into bed and slept more soundly than I had for months.

## A New Call

It is now the fifth day of my retreat. Yes, from that first night I was filled with a sense of all that God had done for me. His call to depth of life and close intimacy was clear and experiential. But then I was moved to take a good hard-headed look at my response to all of this. For three days I struggled with this in prayer, four or five hours a day. What an enormous disparity was happening in my life! Giant input from God, such a mediocre response from me.

The words of the Lord to King David resounded in my ears for a full day. "I called you specifically, crowned you, gave you everything, and if that had not been enough I would have given you twice as much more. Yet what have you done in return?" This seemed to hit my situation squarely. It was as though the Lord had translated this test for me personally and was saying it to my heart: "John, I called you by name and chose you at age fourteen; I led you to the full gift of self by religious vows at age nineteen. From that day on I, your Eternal Partner, was to be the sole object of your total love. I led you step by step to anointing as my priest. I gave you my priestly powers; I gave my people into your hands to lead and feed. I have stepped into your life powerfully so many times, especially in the last two years, again and again inviting you close to me. And if this were too little, I would add so much more. What have you done in return?"

The past was all too clear. My life was a tissue of infidelities; I had turned back. I had immersed myself in the day-to-day rush of teaching and counseling and meetings, spinning my wheels, making contacts, reveling in the flow of fast-paced action. And so the days and weeks went by with little real prayer, little real personal contact with my God. In retrospect my life seemed to be such a surface life, like a stone a lad would skip across the surface of Lake Superior. The years had flowed over me as a mountain stream over stones. Stones, a good image. My heart, a heart of stone, flinty, crusty, impersonal with God, centered on myself, on my pet ideas, my projects, my successes, the feedback from people. A massive infidelity.

This had been a dilemma for me for years: the human impossibility of giving any kind of adequate response to a God who called me to give nothing less than all. I felt my growing shame at such infidelity. Yet I felt incapable of taking any decisive step towards him. The words of the Book of Revelation came home to me, and I prayed on them. It seemed as though they had been spoken to me alone; for a day they echoed through my prayer. "I know what you have done; I know that you are neither cold or hot. How I wish you were one or the other. But because you are neither cold or hot, just lukewarm, I feel like vomiting you out of my mouth."

For days I wrestled with God in desolate prayer, apart from him. I needed so badly his direct touch, his healing grace to melt my heart and move me off dead center. I wrestled with my own prized self-sufficiency. I was forty-seven; I had put my life together; I was a good teacher; I could give love and concern and care to my students and people who needed me. People sought me out. And yet I could not believe in God's great love for me and receive it and respond simply and lovingly to that central Reality of my life. Here all was gift, and I seemed so unmoved. I marveled at how successfully I had kept God at arm's length in my life, how cold and impersonal and objective and intellectual I had been, and above all how active I could be week after week, month after month as the years piled up. A fine way to play it safe and continue in my old days and to avoid the deep intimacy I knew in my bones he was calling me to. I asked God in my helplessness to break through my defenses and penetrate my crust.

Then quite suddenly on the fifth day God did just that. He came crashing through. Just before noon I had a chance conversation with Joe Doyle, a marvelous, warm Jesuit retreat director from New Orleans. He listened and then spoke quite simply to me. "John, God loves you. He wants your whole heart. How hard it is for us, who try to give so much to others, to receive love ourselves and to drink it in and thrill to it and thank God for it. And yet, John, you are a lover at heart. Your vocation is to love this living God. Let it come out of your depth."

I went back to my room in a hurry, blinding back the tears that began to well up from deep within me. Once in my room it all came out: tears, deep tears, cleansing tears, clearing tears, finally joyful tears. Then a growing sense of joy and of expanding spirit and a rising, a wanting to soar riding buoyant thermals. Everything around me seemed changed and became luminous signs of this God's great love. I sensed myself before God, God who was pure Gift, giving himself to me and sharing his very life and joy and all he had with me in my life history.

He, unconditional love, whose ecstasy it is to fill my emptiness and isolation with his fullness. My heart resonated with gratitude and love that came from deep places. I was aware of God present all around me; he, the great atmosphere surrounding me, indwelling in me because he loves me and wants to be near the one he loves as guest, he present in Eucharist and given into my hands as priest.

This God at work for me in the whole world, bringing the miracle of spring for me, for me the warmth of the sun, for me the cool healing waters of lakes and rivers, for me the glory of the sunset; God at work in the fine young people I came to know very well, invading their conscious life and moving into their depths and calling them to personal life with him—and I, the spectator of all this, often even the instrument through which he works; God at work in my life history, the marvel of an early call and then his unwearying return with the insistent call to come closer still. This God whose name is love, source of all life and breath and goodness and beauty, ground of being, granite of it; past all grasp God; he for whom I am created and whom I desire.

Suddenly prayer was easy and poured out of me like a spring that had been at last cut loose from subterranean depths. Now and in the days ahead my prayer periods would go for two hours at a stretch, and this with ease and no strain. I had always been a great clock-watcher in prayer. One firm eye on the minute hand to catch the end of the hour with relief. For the next four days this ease continued to such a point that Peter counseled moderation, "Keep it to an hour." Slowly over days six, seven, eight, the first outpourings, almost too strong a current for me to sustain, moderated to a deep and quiet and steady stream like a river leaving waterfalls and rapids behind in the hills and gliding serenely towards the open sea.

During this time one symbol kept resonating with me. Watching all the activity of a Wisconsin spring, I was struck by the large number of birds: robins, jays, grackles, who mostly hugged the ground and never went above the treetops. Their activity was building nests, yanking worms out of the soil, foraging endlessly for food, and defending their turf. But there were other birds that fascinated me more, especially before a storm. These would soar straight up ecstatically and then ride the wind almost out of sight against the gathering clouds. The swallows became symbols of my own spirit and what was going on in me during the last half of this retreat. I felt a kinship with them, a wanting to soar with them in the boundless sky high above the earth, to ride the free flowing wind, to be an adventurer of the heights. A symbol of the contemplative call.

The last two days of the retreat consolidated the conversion grace. Peter with sure instinct set me praying on the Emmaus journey. And so on a walk along the lake Jesus joined me and told me, "John, how foolish and how slow of heart you are not to believe what is there so clearly in Scripture from the start, that God is love and he loves you as lover. I, the Bridegroom, have said it every possible way I could and finally in my passion and death. Are you some kind of blockhead to miss what is so clear?" Yes, foolish; yes, slow of heart. All this stuck deeply and took the experience I had just undergone and founded it even more deeply on God's revealed word in Scripture.

The final cap was Jesus meeting me along the lake after the resurrection. Peter LeBlanc invited me to become the apostle Peter for a day and take charge of the fishing expedition. When the catch finally came, I sprang into action; John tapped me on the shoulder and said simply, "It is the Lord." I dropped the net, dove in and then swam to the risen Lord on the shore. How would he greet me, I who had responded so shabbily to him in my life? The Lord resolved it so simply; he waded out to meet me, picked me up out of the water, and embraced me. In that strong hug I knew, as Peter knew, that all my past infidelity had been brushed aside and swallowed up by his love. All that was done away with; what remained was his simple question after breakfast, "John, do you love me?"

I would have a lifetime to answer that question. His charge, "Feed my sheep," would be the work of my life.

Along with this movement toward the Lord was an enormous desire to communicate the love of God I felt pulsing in me to the young people I dealt with and to all I met. All sorts of good resolves and projects and plans for the year ahead welled up in me, ways in which I could translate this into life. This love could not be contained; it had to overflow to others.

# 4

# New Horizons, 1974

## Zunil, Guatemala

June, 1974. Little did I know it, but yet another new chapter was about to open up. Concern for the poor and for the so-called Third World served by our Jesuit missionaries had always been part of my life as a Jesuit. In the early years of training, I avidly read the lives of heroes like Francis Xavier, Matteo Ricci, Robert de Nobili, Charles Spinola, John de Brebeuf and Isaac Jogues. These giants of the early Society stirred youthful idealistic dreams. One out of every eight American Jesuits is a missionary. All the way through the fifteen-year training a procession of missionaries came to us and talked of their work: Madeiros of Baghdad, Bernie Hubbard of Alaska, Harry Delaney from Honduras, Paul Dent from India, to name a few. I watched my classmates volunteer and head off for the missions: Renner and Poole and Bernie McNeill to Alaska, Leo Weber to Belize, Bernbrock and Daly for our new mission in Korea. In 1949 I came within a whisker of volunteering for three years of teaching at Sophia University in Tokyo.

After ordination, I had had the great fortune to be a year-long chaplain at Haskell Indian Institute in Lawrence, Kansas. There I lost my heart to young Papagos and Iroquois and Apaches and Blackfeet and Navajos and Cherokees. That year I met one of the finest young people I've ever known, an Iroquois, Dave Herne, a deeply Christian young person, so proud to be an Indian and a Christian. At the end of that year I was much tempted to give several years of my life to the Indian apostolate.

But my first love won, Marquette High School in Milwaukee. I'd loved the past fifteen years there, but something was missing. My world was too tidy, too cozy, too provincial. Yes, I had tried to teach my lads a strong global sense, to give them a care for the hungry and poor of our world; I taught John XXIII's *Pacem in Terris* and Paul VI's landmark *Development of Peoples*. I had read a lot on the Third World; I could spew off statistics. But it was all from books, hardly rooted in my own experience.

In July of 1973 at a Jesuit conference in San Francisco, I was told of a new program planned for the next summer for Jesuit priests and brothers who had completed their training and were working in an active apostolate. It was to be an immersion experience into the poverty of a typical poor Latin American country to create greater personal awareness for the Jesuit and then energize him to bring that awareness back to the people we serve in our parishes and universities and high schools. Reverse mission they called it. This immediately caught my interest. In February, when the letter came from national Jesuit headquarters announcing the "Horizons for Justice Program," it took no longer than thirty seconds to make my decision. It was as if a spark slumbering in my depths had spurted into flame. Intuitively, I knew this was for me.

After a week of orientation and Spanish language classes at Georgetown University, with forty other U.S. Jesuits, I found myself on June 27 winging my way on Pan Am into Guatemala. Two nights later in a Toyota wagon full of Germans, I drove up and over a 10,000-foot mountain pass under a full moon; off to my left great volcanos soared into the night sky, a dramatic landscape unrolling like a dream. At midnight we arrived in our new home; for the next month Zunil would be my base.

A few words about this pueblo. An Indian town of 7,000 people 6,500 feet up in a dramatic river valley of Western Guatemala, Zunil is a farming community where almost the entire population raises corn and vegetables in small family plots on each side of the river and up the sheer mountain sides.

I suppose the first thing that struck me was the poverty of the village. The Indians are industrious people who work their small machetes and hoes six days a week from 6:30 A.M. till 5:00 P.M. Their income: 60-80 cents a day. Their daily diet is corn in various forms and beans. The typical village house has one small room under a thatched or tiled roof, with dirt floor, open fire in the middle, a few small chairs and no windows. There is no green grass around the houses but lots of dirt and mud. Some houses have no doors, and this is cold country. Every night I burrowed into my sleeping bag attired in stocking cap, ski wear, and long sweat socks, with two blankets over me and still shivered in this crisp mountain air.

I soon experienced the shadow that hung over this lovely mountain town. Malnutrition was all too obvious. Thank the corn diet for that. In this town, I was a head taller than anyone else. The local doctor who lived with us told me 80 percent of the young people suffer from one of the three grades of malnutrition and were from 10 to 45 pounds underweight. Because of their weakened condition, these people are set-ups for lung and throat diseases (the greatest killers), for worms and parasites, for dysentery and diarrhea. When a couple marry, they can expect to lose over half their children, many between the ages of two and four. The staggering fact is that 50-65 percent of the young people in this village die before they have really lived.

So much was to happen that summer, and it would change me in ways I could never have foreseen. In my forty-nineth year the affliction of the suffering world south of our border entered for the first time into my bloodstream and invaded my soul. I admit that I fell in love with the gentle Mayan Indian people of the mountain highlands. I became their priest and they became my people. Their affliction became my affliction. Their hunger and malnutrition, their sickness and disease and early death, their illiteracy and marginality, the grievous structural oppression they lived under, in some visceral sense became mine.

A strange thing happened that summer which I regard of utmost importance and now see as a once-only gift of God. During that summer I hardly prayed in any formal sense. No need to. To my intense surprise, I experienced the Lord directly, powerfully, and continually in the poor suffering Mayan Indian. In Masses on open mountainsides, in late night sick-calls to dying Indians, in my first sight of a starving child, in the dramatic beauty of nature, in the gentle eyes of smiling farm people: time after time God moved into my life touching me in a deep way. It was as though Jesus' words in Matthew's Last Judgement account became suddenly direct, experiential. I found this Christ that summer almost at will in my poor neighbor, my oppressed neighbor, my suffering and dying neighbor. "Lord when did we see you?" "John, whenever you found my brother or my sister hungry and thirsty and suffering, there you found me." And so it was in a way I feel powerless to express or describe. All I can do is state it flatly as fact.

As a result of this summer experience, I filled three personal journals. Now ten years later, it's so difficult to select special moments. But here are just a few key experiences from that rich summer.

## Sunday Mass

Sunday morning, June 30. After breakfast I hurry to the sacristy for my first Mass assisting Fr. Siegfried Fleiner, a young German who has been there for nine years: a patient "conscientization" man in the Paulo Friere tradition, one loved by his people. There in the sacristy I'm solemnly introduced to nine little Indian boys in red cassocks and white surplices. Skimpy kids with serious brown faces. At nine sharp we stepped out into the bright sunshine, a perfect mountain highlands morning. Over the fountain in front of the ornate facade of this great colonial church rose Santa Maria, a stunning 14,000-foot volcano.

The procession moved into the church. To the right stood the women and girls, their dresses creating a riot of color with their bright, precise geometric patterning which the Indians weave on hand looms at home. To the left men and boys stood clad in worn and patched clothes. Many were barefoot. To my amazement dogs wandered freely up and down the aisles; as we came to the altar, a pig lumbered out of our way.

Then we were greeted by a burst of lilting song, the exuberant *alegria* came to love. In the sanctuary ahead were a band of guitars, bass, and horns, the boys' choir in red surplices, and the adult choir in motley. The song swelled from hundreds of Indian throats and soared to the ceiling. The sudden beauty and sheer exuberance of it all took my breath away. It was my first experience of vibrant Central America liturgy. A visual and audial overdose.

In Spanish, Siegfried gave the opening blessing, and then *ten piedad de nosotros* (Lord have mercy on us) broke out from one side, rose in response immediately from the other. We sat down as an Indian with great dignity read the Bible readings of the day in the Quiche dialect. Siegfried's sermon, half-Spanish, half-Quiche, was translated by the interpreter. I was moved by the lovely Gelineau psalm at the offertory, by the reverent hush of the whole church at the Eucharistic prayer, by the beautiful Spanish acclamation and the triumphant amen after the Doxology. At Communion time the whole church surged forward as Siegfried and I and two Indians brought the Lord to his people. The women came clad in the rich patterned red of their village, babies swaddled at breast or bundled at back, the gentle, reverent brown faces intense in devotion, and the dwarfling little kids looking up at me and smiling as they receive the Lord. "The Body of Christ," "The Body of Christ," on and on till all are fed. Meanwhile from the hearts of the people soar the Spanish rhythms I learned to love, singing as I had never heard in our U.S. churches.

As I step outside into the bright sunlight and blink at the volcano soaring into the sky, I'm so glad to be here. The Lord's presence is so tangible and continual.

## A Peasant Home Meeting

Monday, July 1. This evening Siegfried invites me to a home meeting at the house of a new Christian, a man who once persecuted Christians in Zunil. After dinner we walked for ten minutes or so through the dirt streets of the town past rows of one-room adobe houses with their red tile roofs. As we step inside the small house, we're warmly greeted by everyone. I'm introduced by Siegfried as Padre Juan and made to feel quite at home in both Spanish and Quiche.

The house is some thirty by fifteen feet, solid, built of native rocks and plastered with rough mortar. Heavy tiles made in the country form the slanting roof, though many homes in our area have only thatched roofs. Yes, a solid house, but I am to find later that it is a death trap in an earthquake. The floor is hard dirt. No beds are visible. Siegfried tells me that the Indians sleep on mats spread on top of the dirt floor. Various pots and pans hang from one wall. Clothing hangs on pegs from another. A fire in the middle of the floor provides warmth and takes care of the tortilla cooking. There are no windows in the house and no chimney. A hole the size of a baseball up in the corner of the wall near the tile roof provides an escape route for the smoke. My eyes smart at first from the layers of smoke. The walls are blackened from the ever-present fire.

The dirt floor tonight is strewn with pine sprigs and boughs. A table sits in the middle of the room with a shrine and little statue of Mary prominently displayed. Two small chairs, some fifteen inches high, like third-grader chairs, are set out for Siegfried and myself.

How stark this typical Quiche home is. And yet this is home sweet home for a family of nine people. In its narrow confines the drama of their lives is played out. No privacy, people on top of people always. Fourteen couples are here tonight for this family meeting and twenty or so little Indian kids everywhere underfoot. A few chickens scratch around in the dirt.

First, Siegfried and I bless this convert's home. The host thanks us, and then we sit in the low chairs. With great dignity our host and his wife serve us with *pan dulce*, a fine sweet roll, and a tin cup of piping hot chocolate. *Muchas gracias*, all around. Then we settle down for the family meeting. The men sit on boards on one side and soberly take up the discussion for the evening. The women squat on the floor on the other side, wrapped in their colorful shawls. The little kids play around the room as kids everywhere do, furtively pee in the corner on occasion, wander around looking into the eyes of the men, move in and out of their mothers' laps.

The subject tonight is the town school and what it's doing for the kids. Siegfried listens far more than he talks; his questions only draw more out of the speakers. His mode is gentle conscientization, making people aware of their own problems, never running ahead of them.

And what a problem the school is! There are over 800 kids of school age in this town; yet the school at most can house 200. There's a big influx into first grade and a real desire for an education. But the teachers are all political appointees, Latinos, who speak only Castilian Spanish, and the kids know only Quiche, their Indian dialect. So the teachers arrive late, leave early, horse around a lot, lecture on Guatemalan history and geography to uncomprehending kids. After a year of this, the boy or girl in the first grade feels he or she is dumb and is not learning a thing. The parents see the reality. And so after a year or two the child either drops out or is pulled out of this losing situation by his parents. Less than two percent in this country ever graduate from eighth grade.

I'm appalled at this; I'm later to learn that this is planned illiteracy. The government intends it. They simply don't want educated Indians. Far better to have a passive, illiterate Indian who will never challenge your rule.

I watch parent after parent gently voice their concern and bewilderment, the men first, then the women. As I study their faces and listen to their natural eloquence, these Indian people begin to come alive for me as individuals with their own cares and convictions and concern for the future of their kids. Siegfried quietly translates for me and cues me into the discussion. I'm fascinated by this world, yet so deeply disappointed.

After an hour which terminated on a resolve to make representation once more to government officials in Quetzaltenango, the province capital, we all rise. Each person in the room comes forward and bids us goodbye, *Muchas gracias, Padre Juan.* To my embarrassment, many kiss my hand as I leave.

As Siegfried and I walk back home and cross the mountain torrent Samala, I'm deeply impressed by the gentle dignity and warm ways of these Mayans. I think I shall be quite at home here this summer. I resolve to make a study of every area of life in Zunil: the health situation, the water, the food, the land, the customs. Siegfried seconds this and pledges his help.

## Midnight Volcano Climb

On July 4, it happened. Aki and Lena, a Swedish volunteer couple who had just adopted a Quiche boy, invited me in for the gringo feast day. We toasted each other with *aguardiente*, illegal Indian white lightning brewed from fruit juice in the mountains. I will regret that toast. And then we talked the evening away about their work with the cooperatives.

Next morning I woke with the sun, took two steps from my collapsible cot, and was smitten by a sudden cramp in the lower tract as though a vise had clamped onto my innards. Abandoning all dignity, I ran for our two-holer and just barely made it. Several minutes later I emerged glad the crisis was over. But it was just a start. Ten minutes later the vise clamped me again, and again the unholy rush! By now the Quiche family on the other side of the wall was watching with great grins and yet concern. Yes, the Aztec two-step. Montezuma's revenge. Dutifully I downed one Lomotil pill to cap this rampant geyser. Five trips and five Lomotil pills later, the whole process finally came to a halt. By noon I'm dehydrated and weak, yet not really aware of how badly dehydrated. Ron and Patricia, a young couple from Toronto who lived on the other side of the wall, and who are recovering from drug experiences and seeking some kind of peace, assure me I've just had the authentic Third World experience.

Then a big mistake. At midnight I hop into the Toyota and join a determined group of Germans led by Indian guides who drive to the foot of Santa Maria and start the ascent of the great volcano. At 3:30 A.M., in the middle of the rain forest, the whole party has to confess that they are hopelessly lost; eight leave, but three Germans and myself, flashlights in hand, head straight up for the summit, path or no path, at times squirming on our stomachs till we emerge from the rain forest. As the sun streaks the east, we switch back up through the pines, onto the murderous slopes of the cone, and up to the summit.

But I had underestimated the dehydration factor. The last steps up the towering cone were pure agony. I honestly thought for a while that I was going to die on the side of Santa Maria. We would stop, gasp for air, let our racing hearts settle down, and begin again. On top at last, we sat exhausted in the morning sun and drank in the stunning view: a solid line of giant cones towering into the sky for 120 miles with Tacana and the other volcanos stretching to the north into Mexico. The very rim of the world. Smoking Santiagito, an active volcano, lay below us. We took pictures and headed for home. I remember the terrible descent. For hours I plodded down like an animal lurching and staggering, my feet raw and blistered, so terribly thirsty that I had only one consuming vision: lying under a tree at the bottom downing the biggest liter of *Cerveza* I could find.

## Too Young to Die

It's now Sunday afternoon and I am healing. Siegfried sends me to the other side of the river to anoint and pray for a young girl who is very sick. I'm met at the door by her father and ushered into the dark one-room dirt-floor adobe. The three-stone fire blazes away filling the house with smoke. Twenty or so family, relatives, and friends stand to one side to greet me. I go over to the other corner and sit down beside the girl. She's only fifteen, yet so small, more like a ten-year old. For three years she has suffered from chronic dysentery and intestinal worms; for months now she has been lying on this mat on the dirt floor. She's taken some medicine the last month or so, but nothing helps now. The catechist Juan tells me that her parents won't let her go to our tiny mission hospital; hospitals for them are a place people go to die. Besides, if you get sick and get well, that's God's will; if you get sick and die, that's God's will; so who needs hospitals? I speak to her in my halting Spanish. Her sorrowful brown eyes follow my every move. I give her the sacrament of the Anointing of the Sick and pray to the Lord to heal her if he would; if not, to give her faith and strength and courage and hope for the trip home.

Then I ask all to pray. The murmur of *Padre Nuestro* rises

from the wretched little casa to the Lord of the hills, the peasant God. Finally I bless this lovely girl whose life is so cruelly being cut off by what is so easily avoidable: the shoes she didn't have—to walk barefoot in this town is to get stomach worms; the pure water she couldn't drink—the water everywhere here is poison; the medicine that wasn't given; the illiteracy and primitive superstition and poverty that ruled out the hospital. I still see the infinite hurt in those fifteen-year-old eyes. They will forever be a part of my life, I know. How one aches for these young. I think of high school girls at our Marquette dances, five or six inches taller, healthy, tanned, brimming with vitality, and my heart aches for the lovely little malnourished kids in my town.

I stand and all twenty people move towards me, shaking hands with me, some kissing my hand, murmuring their thanks to "Padre Juan." I am deeply touched and embarrassed. On the way home, Juan tells me she will most surely die. In the late stages of worms, people usually aspirate or cough up stomach worms. How awful, I think. A week later, while I was away in the capitol, this little girl died and was buried in the cemetery above the town on the same day. Probably with the pathetic little oompah band and the refrain, "Now we have a little *niña* in heaven."

The World Health Organization and UNICEF state that world-wide 15.3 million little kids annually, 42,000 a day, die like this. Conservative estimates peg the number of chronically malnourished at 500,000,000 to 700,000,000 in the Third World. What I saw here was but a window to the wider world. I will never forget it.

Later that same Sunday afternoon Hedwig, an Indian cate-chist, and I pile into the Toyota and drive ten miles or so on a side road up into a different valley, park the car, and then walk for half an hour higher and higher into the mountains. My feet are tender, but we finally arrive at a small village high on a mountain perch. No church anywhere in sight, but we're led to an outdoor altar carefully decorated with sprigs of evergreen, a vine-covered trellis above the altar. Gifts of cabbages and onions and flowers are heaped in front of the altar, first fruits of the fields. Seventy-five or so Indian villagers, colorfully dressed, stand in a wide semicircle around the altar and murmur a gentle welcome to us. Four men, respected leaders in the village and catechists, introduce themselves. They have prepared the altar, will lead the singing, read the Scripture, preach the homily, and in general direct everything.

I vest and greet the people and summon them closer. I look out over my people gathered in this wild aerie and begin in my faltering Spanish *"En nombre del padre ... "* With all my heart, I wish them, *"El señor este con vosotros."* Miguel, head catechist, reads the two readings and the gospel in Quiche and then proceeds to give a sermon. He has a simple, direct intensity and eloquence. Hedwig whispers to me that it's a line-by-line commentary of the gospel centering on the emphasis Siegfried gave in the Zunil Mass that morning. As he talks, I watch the fog fill the valley and creep up the mountainside towards us. Thunder rumbles somewhere above us and then is quiet. I cannot understand a word, so I watch the intent faces of the men and women as they follow Miguel's talk. Only the youngsters fidget, as they do everywhere.

Miguel finally finishes. I go to the altar and there lift the gifts of bread and wine—the joys and sufferings of this people—to the Lord of the mountains and the sky and the stars. Led by the catechists, we sing praise to God *"Santo, Santo, Santo."* They kneel as I take bread and wine into my hands and say the Lord's Last Supper words: "This is my body, this is my blood." Then I bring the Lord to them. Little Indian kids, women in their handwoven crimson Sunday best, the men in their patched Salvation Army clothes come to me, and I place the Lord of the Universe on their tongues: *"El Cuerpo de Cristo."* I marvel again at the gentle eyes, the quiet intensity, the deep reverence of these people. How I love these moments. This Eucharist, high on this wild perch up in the mountains with thunder rumbling, surrounded by those hill people, is so special. Love for them, compassion, deep wishes for these people, all find tongue again and again in the phrases of the Mass and each resonates deeply within me. I give them my blessing and unvest, immensely happy and free. There's no place I'd rather be.

July 12, Friday morning. I'm alone in the parish *casa* before the fireplace copying into my journal significant quotes from the Medellin documents. This landmark 1968 meeting of the South American bishops translated Vatican II spirit into the Latin American experience. This one sentence seems to me to sum up best what I've been experiencing in Zunil for the last two weeks: "Latin America lives under the tragic sign of underdevelopment, a compounding of hunger and misery, illness of a massive nature and widespread infant mortality, of illiteracy and marginality, or profound inequality of income ..."

Suddenly the door bell clangs. Diego, age twenty-eight, father of three, stands there with a big smile on his face. "Padre Juan, will you come over to the church this afternoon for a blessing?" In my halting Spanish, I assure him I will and ask him what the blessing is all about. "Padre", he says with the same smile, "it is for my little *niña* who died last night." "Oh, no, Diego, not your lovely little eleven-year old daughter? This is terrible." Diego's eyes mist over, "Padre, it is God's will. We must not be angry with God; now my family has a little angel in heaven."

I go back into the rectory with fists clenched. I feel like punching out the first window I see. If there is one thing God does not will, I'm sure, it is the needless death of these lovely malnourished children, haunted by the spectre of dysentery and virus. How needless this all is; yet day by day the relentless statistic: two of every three kids of this town die early. I'm sick of burying beautiful little children in stark wooden boxes. Yet I'm staggered somehow at the simplicity of Diego's faith.

So, that afternoon in the silent church, I say the words of consolation over the little crate box, grieving in my heart with Diego. "Eternal rest grant unto this little one; Lord, let your perpetual light shine upon her; I am the resurrection and the life. The one who believes in me will live even if she dies; may the angels lead you home to paradise; may the martyrs come out to welcome you."

After the blessing Diego comes up to me all smiles and thanks me and gives me a *quetzal* bill which I don't at all want to accept and then invites me outside to a surprising sight. A procession was formed into one long line, complete with a six-piece oompah band playing joyous music. The whole troupe takes off, band first tooting away, then the crude wooden box, then Diego and his wife and relatives and mourners. A pitiful, strangely joyous service for the little *niña* who is now "an angel in heaven".

I go back to the rectory torn inside, grieving for Diego and wondering at the staggering faith of the Mayan yet angry at a system that kills as surely as a machine-gun burst. Marxist "opium of the people" thoughts thrust into my mind.

Medellin speaks to me again: "A climate of collective anguish ... an injustice that cries out to heaven."

## The Privileged

Monday, July 15. I leave Zunil via Galpos bus line for a briefing session in Guatemala City. The glorious landscape unrolls before me: the climb to the lookout over the plain of Quatzeltenango up to the volcano, over the 10,000-foot pass on the Pan American highway, through a land of fog and sheep and treeless uplands. Coming into the city from my poor Indian village, I appreciate so much the comparative luxury of the Jesuit high school, Xavier, with its airy rooms, green grass, my own room, clean surroundings, tasteful food, and the view of the mountains from the residence roof.

In the evening I hear the familiar sounds of electric guitars coming from the school and wander into the midst of a group of juniors practicing for a cultural day competition. The boys are outgoing and friendly and accept me easily. Thank God they speak English fairly well, since their professors stress conversational English. And so I meet young Johnny and Ramon and Jorge and Julio and Willy.

The lads tell me about their life: waterskiing on Lake Amiatatlan, their parties and beer drinking, their complaints about schoolwork and boring classes, their work prospect in Panama, the zone they live in and their homes, the music they like, the retreat they went on, their vacations down on the ocean coast, the camping trips climbing Fuego, the fire volcano. I love to tap into the ferment of young life, the enthusiasm for new experience. We discuss a possible exchange of juniors between their school and mine. They play a song for me at earsplitting volume and then fold up their equipment. With a strong invite to watch them sweep tomorrow's competition, the whole pack thunders off into the night on their Hondas.

It's suddenly so quiet. I make my way up to the top of the residence and walk on the roof for over an hour. The sight of these tall, handsome, well-fed lads, so obviously educated, brimming with fun and good spirits, warm with personality, strong in their self-confidence and assurance as they look ahead is almost too much for me coming straight out of my poor mountain village. I think instinctively of my shrimpy, stunted, passive, deprived young people in Zunil with no light at the end of the tunnel. What an enormous inequality! What a chasm separates one from the other! Two different worlds and why should this be so? The sudden juxtaposition of worlds hits deep inside me and clashes unmercifully and tears at me. I walk back and forth across the long roof. I ponder it all, feeling very confused as though I'm holding furious opposites within me, a vast mass of conflicting experiential stuff. I can't sort it all out tonight; yet doggedly I try to solve the questions that keep coming. For an hour I walk that roof praying to the Lord of light as the volcano Fuego glows red on the southern horizon and pours its lava streams into the night. Slowly things settle down; initial anguish gentles down and a confused peace settles in my heart. The Lord of my life is Lord of both Zunil's young and the high school's young. And the poor are his special choice and delight and beloved, that is sure. We are sent to try somehow to fill that gap, that chasm in the course of a human life. The how remains a mystery.

The memory of this night is still very clear to me today. I can feel it in my bones. The effort of the past nine years has been to investigate that how and in one life to do what I can. And there is an abiding sense that the Lord has called me to do what little I can.

## Tikal: Mystery of Time

I love infinity-like stretches. I'm caught and held so often by looking out over blue Lake Michigan stretching to the eastern horizon beyond sight, by the vast Pacific Ocean, by three-billion-year-old Lake Superior Pre-Cambrian rocks, by the star-show wheeling silently before me at night and by the fiery displays of northern lights. These sights nourish me and plunge me into the infinite God.

Each time I read Psalm 90, something resonates deeply in me and springs to life, something awakened early and now more constantly renewed as age comes on so that it seems an endless current running in my depths. Here is the psalm freely rendered.

Lord, you have always been our home.
Before the mountains were begotten
Before the earth and woods were brought forth
      from everlasting to everlasting
      you are God.
A thousand years to you are like one day;
      they are like yesterday, already gone
      like a short hour in the night.
We last no longer than a waking dream.
We are like the grass of the field:
      at dawn it springs up, grows and bursts
      into bloom, by evening it wilts and fades.
Seventy years is all we have, eighty if we are strong
      and most of them are fruitless toil.
Life is soon over and we are gone.
Teach us how short our life is
      so that we may become wise.
Fill our daybreaks with your constant love
      so that we may sing and be glad
      all the days of our life.

The mystery of time. My own life so quickly passing like the wake behind a ship; and yet cupped in the hands of an ever-lasting God for whom time is meaningless.

It's July 17, and I embark on what turns out to be a profound experience of time. I'm riding a DC-3, bouncing over mountains and the endless green carpet of Peten rain forest. We bank suddenly and there before me are five great stone hulks standing clear above the jungle: Tikal, the ancient Mayan religious center. We land on a gravel runway, lunch at the Jaguar Inn, and camera and all, hustle out to the most famous of the Mayan ruins, Tikal, the wonder of the world. Monkeys chatter through the trees above me, wild turkeys and brilliant parrots fly on ahead shrieking, a friendly horned deer nuzzles my knee at a temple. And then I walk into the sprawling central plaza of Tikal. Twelve-foot steles commemorating leaders of the theocracy loom along the north side of the plaza. The face of each has been defaced. The earliest stele here is dated 292 A.D.

Immediately in front of me, the great Jaguar temple soars 145 feet into the sky. To my left in tier upon tier of terraced stone masonry 200 feet wide looms the North Acropolis. Halfway up is the giant face of the Mayan favorite, the rain god, Chok. To my right, the South Acropolis rises, stone temple upon stone temple. Behind me on this great plaza is temple 2, equal in size and facing the Jaguar temple.

This central plaza is the very heart of Tikal. I'm told that the oldest radio-carbon dating of these ruins is 269 B.C. and the latest is 869 A.D.: 1,100 years! Also below my feet is ninety-five feet of buried ruins. A stupendous site, almost impossible for me to comprehend. Mayan Indians living here in the jungle found and quarried the limestone and began building temples to their gods under the direction of their priestly ruling class: all this 300 years before Jesus was born. Layer upon layer succeeded each other over 1,100 years, until these present majestic structures stood stark against the sky. Around the year 900, this sprawling ceremonial city, able to accommodate 250,000 religious pilgrims, was suddenly abandoned for who knows what reason and the whole civilization trekked off to the Yucatan. Marauding bands pillaged the abandoned temples. And then the giant trees of the jungle moved in, slowly covering them with a carpet of green. And Tikal slumbered, lost to history.

I climb the steep, worn steps of the Jaguar temple, hanging grimly onto the heavy chain for support. I gain the top and the room where the high priest carried out harvest sacrifices. I turn to a stunning scene: the massive southern acropolis, three temples towering above the green Peten jungle, the plaza below crawling with ant-like tourists. I capture it on film, then descend to the great plaza, trying to digest it all.

I'm almost fifty years old, very aware I'm at midlife passage. My life is busy with teaching and learning and the problems of people in trouble and teenagers advancing on life and trying to lay hold of some meaning. I'm enthusiastic, caught up with a whole set of projects and dreams that I want to implement. At times I work too compulsively and lose perspective.

And yet here in the Peten rain forest time suddenly stands still. I'm brought up short in the great plaza by the sight of soaring structures built by flesh and blood mortals 2,000 years ago, monuments of a great civilization that once flourished and reached its peak and vanished into history. The stele of sixth-century powerful priests, their noses broken and defaced when they died, peer down at me. My fifty years of life seem suddenly so paltry. The projects that teem in my head, all I still want to do, that I get worried about and frustrated at, seem suddenly so insignificant as I view Tikal. I marvel at this Mayan world and its stone symbols. I think of the men of Maya and their exact calendars, the astronomers who pondered the course of the stars in the tropical nights and constructed sacrifice rooms so exact as to catch the once-a-year conjunction of constellations. I think of the Spirit of God riding time like a river who spoke to ancient Mayans and moved in their depths and awoke them to praise and to clothe their praise in these mighty monuments. *Sursum corda* in stone. Cathedrals of the jungle. Reverence and admiration and praise and prayer well up within me and struggle for expression. I could sit here for hours.

About 9:00 I wander away from the camp and walk the airstrip alone. At 10:30 the generators go off and the whole camp is plunged abruptly into darkness. The night is cloudless, the sky inky black, and the stars so clear and close it seems one could pick them out of the sky. I'm overwhelmed by the star-show and walk and walk filling my eyes with the glow of the jungle night. I pray to the Lord of the universe and the Lord of man's history with words that start and halt and never seem adequate, a dumb sense of praise rising in me, incapable of any right expression.

Phrases of psalms surface:

Lord how majestic is your name in all the earth.
When I look at the heavens, the work of your
        fingers, the moon and the stars you have
        established—
What are we that you care for us?
The heavens tell the glory of God,
        the sky proclaims his handiwork,
Night declares the knowledge to night,
        their voice goes to the end of the world.
To you, O Lord, I lift up my soul.
Glory be to the Father, Son and the Holy
        Spirit
As it was in the beginning is now and ever
        shall be,
Amen.

And so I go back to my cabin, kill two cockroaches, and sleep in the tropic heat. It's hard to believe I'm here, but I'm so grateful. Tikal is truly a wonder of the world. Once again, more graphically than even before, I am confronted with the mystery of time.

## Awakening to Structures

Friday, July 19. Five of us Jesuits journey into zone 5, the poor zone, to the two-story house of Cesar Jerez, S.J. His quarters are poor and crowded. Cesar is a native Guatemalan, a Ph.D. from the University of Chicago in sociology and political science. Over the years he has profiled in great detail the exact power structure of his country. During this spring's election, he had to go underground for fear of his life. He simply knew too much.

This very intelligent, articulate man, gentle in manner, but with eyes that burn, answers our questions and cues us into the history and present situation of the country we have come to love. His four-hour briefing highlights the crucial problem of land reform; the 1954 United Fruit-CIA overthrow of elected President Arbenz; the reality of right-wing death squads; the peasants' prospect of starving; their inferior education; U.S. multinational corporations' exploitation and huge profits; the ever-present "fight Communism" excuse to justify much of the above; U.S. arms in the hands of the military, plantation owners, and death squads; grassroots group organization rather than violence as the key to the future.

I see Cesar's briefing fleshed out in a hurry. That night my young friends Ramon and Willy from the Jesuit high school come by to talk. Ramon tells me about his uncle, a labor leader who lived two houses down from him. The uncle got into hot water with the ruling powers over a TV interview nine days before. Three days later, as Ramon was getting up in the early morning, he looked over at his uncle's house, saw a large van drive up and men with machine guns pile out and rush in. He heard six short bursts of machine gun fire; the men drove off into the sunrise. Ramon ran into the house and found his uncle dying in a pool of blood at the foot of the stairs, his body ripped by the bullets. *Mano blanco* death squad. Ramon is an angry young man, determined to make change. I ask him if he is afraid. He tells me that "they" are more afraid of a young person with ideas than he is of them. Willy says you must do what you believe in even if it means your life. There is a marked social conscience in both young men: they feel deeply for the poor; they want to spend their lives to better conditions; some of their classmates refer to them as "Communists." What will become of their dreams?

### Sister Jane Buellsbach, M.D.

It's Monday, July 29, and I'm in western Guatemala visiting Maryknoller Jane Buellsbach who operates out of the San Marcos area. Jane is a medical doctor, graduate of St. Louis University, a veteran missionary who has established innovative health systems, first in Jacaltenango and now in San Marcos. In the afternoon we take her VW up into the mountain heights on roads that progressively deteriorate until we reach our destination.

First, we visit a dear old Indian woman with cataracts and fearful of a hospital stay, then an old man dying of congestive heart trouble compounded by TB and malnutrition. Jane tells me that the hills are filled with thousands of these people, many dying of TB.

Then I go to a grade school where lovely Indian children gather round me shyly smiling. I have them read to me out of their notebooks, and suddenly they come to life and sing their songs. As they clown around, I take pictures of the whole group. Jane appears and takes me over to an Indian woman she has been examining. The woman is in her late twenties, eight months pregnant, just returned from the coastal region where she's been picking coffee on the *fincas* or plantations. On her back she's carrying a three-year-old dying of malnutrition and now starvation. Jane slowly unwraps the little child. I'm shocked by what I see: a puny child, pitifully thin, eyes shut, blood sores on her chin and face, feet deformed from vitamin deficiency, a line of red sores all the way down from the middle of her chest. Jane holds up the child's arm; off the bone hangs a translucent bag of skin and tissue. Jane says matter of factly, "John, this girl will die. Maybe, just maybe, if we put her in the hospital for six weeks and build her up, we might save her, but I doubt it." Here in the mountains she will simply die. This happens all the time, especially during the annual flux out of the hill country when thousands are trucked down to work on coastal plantations for eighty cents a day. Jane carefully wraps the child and goes off for her two-hour teaching lesson with the health promoters.

I stand there speechless and then stumble off by myself for an aimless walk into the mountains. Fog cuts up into the ravines and spills over the ridges. Afternoon thunderheads are rolling in and thunder growls above. The sight of this child tears at my consciousness and burns deep within me. It is like a living wound. I walk on past a little farm and talk with the Indian farmer. He shows me his pride and joy, a five-day-old goat, and his scrawny chickens and his patch of corn. Orchids grow by the side of his one room house. I walk on for two hours trying to digest what I've just seen. Anguish struggles inside me. That little child, a tragedy that should never happen in our world. It is the dark shadow that hangs over this dramatic landscape like a poised sword. And yet this is commonplace all across Mexico, Central America, India, Africa.

After two hours I calm down a bit. We drive back to the rectory. I'm staying in Fr. Ed Moore's room. After my wretched hut in Zunil, his room is palace. I enjoy a shower, turn on the electric blanket (we're up 7,200 feet) and luxuriate in the warmth. My eye catches a page of print under a glass on Ed's desk and I read it once, twice. It is the famous statement of Belgian Cardinal Suenens "Why Am I a Man of Hope in These Days?"

Slowly it sinks in. This is the way Ed copes with all the misery he lives with daily. I'm privileged to glimpse another human being's foundation in faith, that by which he lives and works even with buoyancy and good humor. This statement of Suenens becomes a favorite, the rock bottom foundation of my hope in trying to forge a world where inequity is no more, where justice and peace have a chance.

"Why are you a man of hope in these days?

"Because I believe God is new every morning, I believe God is creating the world today, at this very moment. He did not just create it in the long ago and then forget about it. That means that we have to expect the unexpected as the normal way God's providence is at work.

"The unexpected of God is exactly what saves and liberates us from determinism and the sociologism of gloomy statistics about the state of human affairs in the present. The unexpected, since it comes from God, is something coming out of his love for us, for the betterment of his children. I am hopeful, not for human reasons or because I am optimistic by nature, but because I believe that the Holy Spirit is present in his Church and in the world even if people don't know his name. I am hopeful because I believe that the Holy Spirit is still the creating Spirit, and that he will give us every morning fresh freedom, joy, and a new provision of hope, if we open our soul to him.

"I believe in the surprises of the Holy Spirit. The Council was such a surprise and Pope John was another. They took us aback. Why should we think that God's imagination and love might be exhausted?

"Hope is a duty, not just a nicety. Hope is not a dream but a way of making dreams become reality.

"Happy are those who dream dreams and are ready to apply the price to make them become true!"

## Goodbye and Painful Reentry

Sunday, August 4, my last Sunday in Zunil. After an early breakfast, Janet, a sixty-two-year-old Peace Corp veteran, and I drive down the mountain gorge to early Mass at La Estancia and then back up the mountain to the main church for the 9:00 AM. Mass I love so much. One final time we walk in procession in the dazzling sunshine. Volcano Santa Maria soars over the fountain and village square. We turn to enter the church. That great splash of color of the women in their crimson Sunday best and the whole congregation singing those lilting Spanish songs greet us. My red-robed Indian boys smile at me from the choir as we approach the altar. I relish every part of this last parish Eucharist. Later I give the Body of Christ, *El Cuerpo de Cristo* on and on to so many. I feel deeply that these are my people, my flock.

After we finish, Siegfried asks me to say a few words in my halting Spanish. So I thank these people for kindness to me, their accepting me and my fumbling Spanish, for their warm hospitality. I tell them that Zunil and its people will always be close to my heart and remembered in my Masses wherever I go. I sit down while the translator thanks Padre Juan in the name of the pastor, the church council, and all the people. Then Siegfried whispers, "John, I think some of the people wish to say goodbye and thanks to you. Go out to meet them." I'm flabbergasted as the whole parish comes up, little old women, young people, mothers with their children, older men, and little kids to give me a gentle Indian *abrazo* and murmur their thanks with touching dignity. On and on this goes, and I can hardly believe it. An overwhelming experience of this final day. This too I shall never forget. Half of my heart I will leave in this pueblo with these gentle people. I feel so blessed by the Lord who sent me here. "Blessed are you poor; of such is God's Kingdom."

A final breakfast with the staff, some last pictures, a round of goodbyes, and on over the mountain pass to the capital city. My Jesuit companions, twenty of them, from Salvador, Nicaragua and Honduras are there to greet me. Cesar Jerez debriefs us for two days. Then a jet to Chicago O'Hare and a final debriefing with input from the Peruvian and Mexican groups. Final good-byes and then home to Milwaukee by sunset. This has easily been the best summer of my recent life. Little do I realize how much I have been changed and will change.

Reentry. Friends had predicted I would have culture shock going into the Central American and then into the Indian culture. But that was nothing compared to the culture shock I experienced on my return home. It was a raw experience that took me by complete surprise.

I was relieved to be home. I had lost twenty-five pounds due to dysentery, still had a few intestinal bugs biting me, and was very tired from months of coping with a flood of new experiences. My first day home, I drove down to Lake Michigan and put my arms in its refreshing waters again; then I took a leisurely drive through Shorewood's lovely eastside homes. There, as the evening summer sun slanted across manicured lawns, I watched dads and moms in Bermudas out watering flowers and grass, school-age kids, tall, bright, well-tanned and healthy, riding bikes up and down curving driveways. An idyllic scene, but all I could see were my scrawny Indian kids, a foot shorter, wretchedly thin, malnourished, carrying stomach worms, going to bed on dirt floors in the cold in single room adobe houses, cut off from an education by planned illiteracy. An enormous abyss separated that world from this suburban world, where dogs and cats live better than Third World kids. Strange to say, the sight of those healthy kids was almost too much for me to bear. I jerked the car out of there and headed home in a hurry, feeling vastly troubled.

The next afternoon was far worse. While in Mayfair, a near-by shopping center, I stopped at the indoor ice rink and watched the scene: thirty or forty young people were joyously skating to flowing melody; at one end five or six figure skaters were doing routines and jumps and younger kids played tag and pursued each other—all healthy well-fed kids, firmly muscled, pictures of glowing health. Suddenly a wave of emotion surged up from deep inside, tears filled my eyes as the inequity of all this hit me. All I could think of were the scrawny kids I had lived with and loved, the gentle people of the Guatemalan hills. I just had to get out of there and leave that place fast before I broke down. On the way home, I marveled at the intensity of my reaction.

Over the days and weeks ahead slowly these raw feelings subsided and I began to achieve an uneasy peace in affluent American life. But I knew that my narrow horizons of Milwaukee and Marquette High and the U.S. ways of thinking and living had been forever blown. I would no longer be at home in affluent America. My horizon now would be the world and our globe. The astronauts' picture of the earth from space would be my favorite picture. A twentieth century icon.

Back in 1955, after a tough year studying theology in rural Kansas, ten minutes after finishing my theology oral exam, I sat down and had my first cigarette in eleven years. I told myself I'd smoke for relaxation just that summer and stop on my return in September. A real mistake. Twenty years later I was smoking two and a half packs of Alpines a day and was a real addict. A smoke first thing in the morning; on awakening in the middle of the night, a cigarette; in any pressure situation, a cigarette; in any relaxing situation, a cigarette. I suffered two or three bad colds a year and approached each chest x-ray with trepidation. "Was this the year they would spot the shadow?" Yes, I tried pipes, candy, gum, cutting down, and nothing worked. I had resigned myself to living and dying with smoking, no chance of quitting. Impossible.

It's late May 1975 and I'm sitting on a bench in the evening starting my eight-day retreat at Oshkosh, Wisconsin, looking out at Lake Winnebago. The thought suddenly struck me, "I'm spending more on cigarettes than a poor Indian family has to live on for a whole year. If I'm consistent at all with what I've been teaching and giving to people, why not quit smoking, and do it now." This surprised me, since I brought two cartons to hold me through the retreat. My second thought, "Nobody ever stops during a retreat; it would simply ruin the retreat." A half-hour later I bemusedly told my retreat director, an Irishman from Canada, about my crazy idea; his laconic comment was, "Well, you might give it some thought." And so I found myself quite unexpectedly going to the room of Fr. Bill Brennan, favorite competitor on the tennis courts, and giving him both cartons of Alpines. "I won't be using these; take them." His comment was perfect. "You'll never do it." Just what I needed.

And so I stopped cold turkey. That was my last cigarette. And quitting wasn't too bad, far less than I had expected. I got through the first couple of days; the retreat went well. A few weeks later I experienced a ravenous hunger in midafternoon, plus several completely unusual explosions of temper over trivialities, and that was it. In a year I had lost any desire for smoking. I marveled at this whole process. So unexpected, yet so good. And my doctor cheered.

# 5

## Guatemala Revisited

### San Lucas Food Riot

It's now the summer of 1975. I knew when I returned to Milwaukee that I simply had to share this Third World experience with my Marquette students. And so we planned an awareness work-volunteer summer and lined up five fine high school seniors who were eager to go. San Lucas Toliman mission on the shores of Lake Atitlan, I found out, welcomed volunteer workers and had just finished a small facility to house them. With remarkable luck, I ran into Fr. Greg Schaeffer and Sr. Sandra Spencer from New Ulm, Minnesota, and they urged me to come and bring my boys. So we flew in on Pan Am and took up residence at the very progressive mission, one of the show spots in the country for imaginative grass roots development in the spirit of Schumacher's *Small is Beautiful*.

July 11 was a day my boys and I would never forget. A prenote to this experience. Corn is the staple of an Indian family's diet. A father and mother and four kids need eight pounds of corn daily for the family tortillas and tamales. Ordinarily the price of corn in the village is 11 cents a pound. One Indian father in our area working from dawn until dusk on the coffee or sugar cane *fincas* gets paid anywhere from 80 cents to $1.25 a day. That means an Indian family can afford meat like chicken only once a week or every two weeks. So there is widespread protein deficiency, which is malnutrition. That leaves very little or no money for medicines or other expenses. It's a precarious existence on the edge of subsistence, and death is a familiar reality.

But now a new element. It's the end of the corn season. A country-wide shortage of corn gives corn speculators in the city their golden chance; they drive the price up to 16 cents and more per pound. When this happens, little children die in Indian homes. To blunt this crisis, a government source called Indica sent a truckload of corn to our village square selling corn at 13 cents a pound. So on Friday a line three blocks long forms in the village square. Colorfully garbed women with infants slung on their backs or suckling at their breasts wait patiently in the morning sun for their portion. By mid-morning panic sweeps this long line: the government supply will run out soon. Women begin to clamor and shout and push relentlessly forward to get the last of the grain. The lives of their children are at stake. A wave of women surges toward the building. The little children and babies cry and scream. A terrible sight. A food riot. The ragtag police force and government helpers move in and establish order. An official announces over a bullhorn the end of the sale and the empty truck drives out of town. Hollow-eyed mothers stare into space and then slowly turn home to face their hungry families.

Fr. Greg and the boys and I return to the rectory, shaken by what we have seen. Greg tells us that this is only the start; next year and the following years will be far worse. With the oil shortage worldwide, fertilizer costs will triple, corn yield will drop, prices will rise with inflation. He predicts wide-spread famine in the highlands.

That afternoon the Guatemalan City newspapers come in. Front page pictures show long lines at Amatitlan and other towns, vivid evidence of the food crisis. That night I pick up *The Miami Herald* and look at the headlines: U.S. Expects Record Corn Harvest This Year. Banner crops and great surpluses are predicted in the farm belt states. The articles detail how much of this corn will go to feed livestock so that we can eat Grade A beef in our steaks. I sit there speechless. What an incredible world we live in. This morning a food riot in my town; this evening a glut in my home country. My boys and I are shaken;

we'll never forget what we saw. It's a window of awareness into our globe. The U.S. is truly an island of plenty in an ocean of want, an oasis in a desert of hunger and malnutrition. That night I celebrated Eucharist for my lads in my room in the rectory. I picked up bread and said over that bread: "This is my Body," and gave the Lord to these fine lads. Jesus, of all the ways he could possibly come to us, has chosen bread. The Eucharist and world hunger. May we who have, multiply our loaves and fishes as the Lord did and help us feed the multitudes.

## The Finca System

The distinguishing element of my second summer in Guatemala is experiencing the *finca* system. San Lucas lies at the foot of a volcano, up 5,000 feet, and on the shores of Lake Atitlan, described by Huxley as one of the most beautiful lakes in the world. Great coffee *fincas* surround the town and march down the mountainside to the coast; on the plateau above us one big landowner owns twenty million dollars worth of prime farm land. He uses contour farming on the rich volcanic land and employs a host of peasants at the usual starvation wages. Further down the mountainside lie great sugar cane holdings and a processing plant. Down on the coastal plain sprawl the big cotton producing *fincas* and, to my surprise, huge ranches grazing beef cattle. Coffee is a land-wasting crop. Coffee beans grow on shoulder-high bushes spaced apart under high trees for shade. Thus the best land of the country is taken for an export crop of no known nutritional value and shipped to developed industrial countries like Germany, Holland, Belgium, Britain, the U.S., and Canada. This protein-poor, malnourished country grows more than enough beef to sustain its people, but most of it is shipped to our hamburger chains so that we can protein overdose. The *finca* system, with its export cropping explains the poverty of this country. Three percent of Guatemalan society owns 80% of the farmable land in the country. and that three percent lives in great wealth. The 90% peasant population struggles on postage-stamp farms or works the *fincas* for the usual starvation wages. A system of widespread oppression, a vast inequity with no end in sight, held in place by guns which are everywhere in sight and largely U.S. imported.

Saturday, July 26. Fr. John Goggin, a Minnesota farm "boy" assigned to the *finca* apostolate, invites two of us on a trip into San Bernardino *finca*. We spend an hour loading our Toyota van to the gills with bags of corn, with medicine, Pepsi and other materials. Julio, the paramedic, Jorge, the driver, Cruz, the eighteen-year-old Indian catechist in training, John, Steve from Fox Point and I perch on top of corn bags and take off 2,500 feet down the mountain road. We turn through the gate of St. Theresa *finca*. (I wonder by what irony all the grim *fincas* are named after saints.) We go through flatlands, past meadows, and then up steep grades through the forest. We splash across a mountain river thanks to four-wheel drive and pause to look down a chasm at a 150-foot waterfall. The roads get narrow and bumpier as we climb wild ridges. Brilliantly colored parrots fly over forest tops.

Finally after two and a half hours of bouncing, we descend into a flat plain surrounded by mountains. To the right we see the lovely home of the *finca* owner: a sprawling house with finely carved wooden doors approached from a long lawn, palm trees, a gorgeous red flowering tree in front of the house. A swimming pool is next door. They tell me that this *finquero* is very wealthy and spends four months a year traveling in Europe. When in the country, he drives up the coast road in his red sports car to check with his foreman. With a .45 on his hip, he arrogantly strides around the *finca*. The Indians claim he has an armory of weapons in his basement as threat to any disturber. By law he is required to pay a living wage, provide schooling and medical care as well as adequate housing. But none of this avails. Eighty cents a day is standard pay on this *finca*. If an Indian father complains too loudly or insists on justice required by law, the Indian is found in the forest with a bullet in his head. The foreman and his goon squad see to that. The Indians claim that someday they will stop him on the coast road and end his cruelty.

We drive a half-mile further into the worker settlement. The contrast is striking. Squalor is the word here. A wretched set of single-room wood huts perch on a mud base, crowned with corrugated roofing. Home-sweet-home for the Indian mother and the five dirty children who come out to greet us. Kids are all over the place. A little lad with a swollen belly comes shyly up beside me. John Goggin says simply, "Malnutrition and an advanced case of stomach worms." We bring in the bags of corn, the Pepsi and the other materials and distribute them to the families. People tell us that the *finquero* provides no schooling for their kids, no medical care, and wages few can live on. Julio, our paramedic, makes the rounds of the sick. We come to an open door where a woman sits nursing her baby; flies are all over the baby's face and on the child's closed eyelids. A stinking creek flows in front of the *casa*. Kids with no pants and swollen bellies play around us. Steve, from the wealthy suburb of Fox Point, is revolted by all this. He's had enough and wants to leave.

After some sandwiches and beer, we discuss what we've seen with John Goggin. John chooses to be positive and spends much time working with the *finca* owners, building good will and nudging them to care for their people. But progress is very slow. In reality it's a hopelessly oppressive system of rampant injustice that sprawls across Central and South America.

Around eight, we ring a bell and out of the darkness come Indian people into the old wretched building where coffee is dried. There by the lights of our jeep, with a single sputtering candle, I have a Mass for the people. Aloft at consecration time, I raise the Body of Christ, he who is called savior of his people, liberator from sin and death, our hope and resurrection. This Jesus who takes away the sins of our world I give to the Mayan Indians as they come up: "*El Cuerpo de Cristo.*""

As we bounce back over the moon-drenched roads and climb to San Lucas with the great volcano soaring overhead, I think of the salvation Jesus came to give, of the liberation this savior pro-mises, of the Kingdom he brings where justice and peace must rule. Liberation theology makes more and more sense now. Structural change must come, a mandate of the gospel. And to be authentic, the church must prophetically lead the way.

## Earthquake

I was back teaching at Marquette when, on February 6, 1975, tragedy struck Guatemala. At three in the morning the earth shuddered convulsively as a lethal earthquake rolled across the Guatemalan mountain highlands. Some 100 after-shocks followed in the days ahead until quiet resumed. The capital city, hard hit itself, reeled in disbelief as the grim statistics poured in from the countryside. For days the death toll jumped by thousands until the extent of the disaster was clear: 23,000 people dead, mostly Indians in the highlands country; 76,000 injured, 6,000 very seriously with broken backs and punctured lungs and spinal injuries; 250,000 homes reduced to rubble; one million people homeless. It was Guatemala's worst disaster. Nations of the world quickly rallied to help the stunned populace with supplies, food, medicine and building materials.

Because of teaching duties, I could not get away until Easter vacation. Then, funded by a local foundation, I flew into Guatemala City, camera in hand, to film the disaster. As we drove into the city, ruined adobe buildings were everywhere; rubble and collapsed masonry lay over the streets, bridges were closed, makeshift houses of cardboard and tin were everywhere; tent cities sprawled over the landscape; the frantic effort to rebuild before the rainy season in the late April was in full swing. Liceo Xavier, the Jesuit high school where I stayed, was a shocker. Four floors of this modern school building had accordioned into one floor. The Jesuit faculty huddled together in makeshift quarters at the other end of the campus.

The next day Luis and Jose, Xavier friends, picked me up in their VW and we went on a two-day photo tour of the earthquake damage. The province of Chimaltenango north of the city was the hardest hit, so we headed there. We surveyed first Chimaltenango City, a tangle of leveled houses and churches and public buildings where 900 people had died. Then we turned off the Pan American highway onto a gravel road up and up to a mountain ridge. At the lookout to the south, we took pictures of fold after fold of mountain sides gashed white by landslides, mute testimony to the power of the killer quake.

Then we plunged down into a large canyon with great rock and sand slides all around us. In places the road was closed, so via switchbacks we worked our way up out of the canyon until quite suddenly we were at St. Martin, a long strung-out village. We walked this town from one end to the other, desolation as far as the eye could see. Every adobe house in the town was reduced to rubble. Piles of masonry were everywhere covered by six inches of dust.

We spent time with a middle-aged Mayan Indian outside the wreckage of his home. With vivid gestures he described the sudden down-up thrust of the earth. He told us he had seconds to get out of his adobe house before the rocks and heavy tile came crunching down. How he got out in the darkness he still doesn't know. He lost six of his loved ones in those few moments. Hopelessly, he looked at the rubble of his house and shook his head.

Nine hundred people died in this one little town, 3,000 in the surrounding area. San Martin was perhaps hardest hit of all the province villages. Damage was total.

Jose and Luis and I went over to the great colonial church and photographed the ruins. This once lovely church was so utterly destroyed that only the shell of outside walls were still standing. Giant chunks of masonry were piled one on another on the church floor and in front of the facade. We climbed all over these, took pictures, and then ate our sandwiches and drank some beer. So difficult to comprehend how complete the devastation was in the highlands. I imagined myself awakening at three in the morning, feeling the shuddering earth, somehow or other scrambling in terror out that door as tile and rock thudded around me, as my family died screaming before me. Then the frantic effort to pull away rubble and free screaming loved ones, only to realize that it was hopeless, as the life of my family slipped away. Too much.

And then, unbelievably, as we sat there having lunch, a priest and server and some worshippers filed through the rubble to the main altar and began to celebrate mass in the ruins. "*En nombre del Padre.*" "*Yo Confieso.*" "*El Cuerpo de Cristo.*" We watched from a distance and then drove out of town through chest-high rubble. On the edge of the town a bulldozer churned up clouds of dust moving the debris. Volunteers from neighboring Mexico were hard at work erecting woodless homes. Nearby was a new tent compound. CARE was there with a strong effort, distributing food and blankets and plywood and corrugated roofing. The Salvation Army was much in evidence as well, doing what they could. Guatemala was struggling gamely to get back on its feet.

Numbed by all this suffering, we drove to the parish, San Lucas Toliman, where I was to spend Holy Week. Luckily San Lucas was not hard hit. The people, however, spoke in awe of their great lake (11 by 16 miles) dropping five or six feet in the first tremor as though some gate in the depths had suddenly opened. Up above the cliff on the plateau and through the province of Solola, however, there was widespread damage. Greg and the staff told me that, for the last two months, 200 of the workers trained by the mission had fanned out over the whole area bringing health care, food, and building materials to people in need and were training people to build new earthquake-proof houses, using barbed wire and wood and adobe and corrugated roofing. Greg and his staff were exhausted; these Holy Week days were their first rest in two months.

We celebrated Holy Week as I've never seen it celebrated before. The Indians, under the leadership of the nature confraternities, staged the entire passion and death of Jesus in unforgettable fashion. In the plaza jammed with people, Jesus was crucified before our eyes; at noon the great cross was raised in hushed silence; at 3:00 P.M., Indians took the body of Jesus from the cross with the utmost reverence and placed it in an elaborate glass casket. Then the casket, borne by ten Indian men and accompanied by a solemn drumbeat wound its way through the town. All Friday morning groups of Indians had labored hour after hour to fill the streets with elaborate, richly colored sawdust street-paintings. A group effort, highly artistic, destined to exist for only an hour, a moment of glory, till the procession bearing the body of the Lord passed over it, scattering the sawdust into disarray. On into the evening and through the long night, this procession passed through the silent streets of the village. To be an Indian in this town was to experience the passion of Jesus and to relive it. Against the backdrop of all the suffering and death this poor country had been through since early February, this Good Friday had a special poignancy for me. The passion of Jesus yesterday and today. I thought of the Peruvian liberation theology crucifix: the Indian figure in woodcut, the Jesus who bleeds and bleeds and never dies: Passion of Christ forever.

Easter morning. Fr. Greg and the whole staff processed through the street and into the church to celebrate the Lord's resurrection. "Alleluia, the Lord is truly risen!" After Mass, we drove up along the cliffs to Godinez on the plateau above. Here where two months ago people were crying hopelessly amid the rubble of their town, new houses are in construction everywhere, rubble is being removed, and there in the square a marimba is playing joyous songs of the Lord's resurrection.

*Guatemala en pie*, Guatemala on its feet. Yes, I will return to Milwaukee, talk to groups, show these slides, raise money for reconstruction. But these ten days have hit me on a very deep level. I will never return to Guatemala, it seems now. But these three trips have been most sobering. It's like yanking the bandage off the world's suffering (so carefully concealed from most of us) and peering steadily into the wound. I have been changed, and changed for good.

## Postscript on Guatemala

At this point it would be well to add a postscript on the Third World chapter of my life. Little did I know how much these three immersion experiences would change me. They set me on a search and a course that lasted for ten years and may well last a lifetime. For fifteen years I had been very happy in the world of my high school, but now in retrospect my school seemed a secure little backwater. These experiences forever exploded my horizon. Guatemala was the window to the wider world where one-half of the world's family goes to bed hungry at night, where 750,000,000 people are seriously malnourished, where 15.3 million kids between the ages of one and five die yearly of largely preventable causes: 42,000 a day.

Never again would I be completely at home in my high

school environment. The great heroes of the Third World became my personal heroes: Brazilians Dom Helder Camara of Recife, Pedro Casaldaliga of Mato Grosso, Cardinal Arns of Sao Paolo; Arch-bishop Romero and Rutilio Grande of El Salvador, Cesar Jerez of Guatemala. New words came into my active vocabulary such as: conscientization, *communidades de base*, preferential option for the poor, grass roots development, export cropping, land reform, structural injustice, the new international economic power, transnational corporations, the Medellin documents of 1968, liberation theology, and much else. Avidly I read the great liberation theologians, Gutierrez of Peru and Sobrino of Salvador and Boff of Brazil. They gave tongue and form and theological expression to my experience and my reflection on the gospel and what it was calling us to do.

I felt a deep call to bring this awareness to the middle- and upper-class students and parents and Jesuits. Over the next nine years I taught courses to sophomores and seniors on global awareness, on structural injustice, on simplicity of lifestyle and a commitment to justice in today's world, on war and peace and the arms race. For five more summers we sent groups of seniors to Guatemala, till the violence under General Lucas Garcia became a danger to our lads. Two final groups went to Ecuador to work summers at Fr. John Halligan's famous center for shoeshine boys in Quito. For years I ran a Bread for the World organization and a social issues homeroom for upperclassmen, disseminating information, sponsoring hunger weeks, sending money to Catholic Relief Services and San Lucas and Quito. In 1985, five of our college grads worked in Quito with Fr. Halligan; many have gone to Peace Corps and Jesuit Volunteer Corps and refugee work.

Yet this work of global awareness, this labor of uncovering structures of oppression, this challenge to transnational corporations, to our foreign policy and its apparatus, to the ultimate structure of injustice, to the arms race and its senseless product of nuclear terror, this debunking of the whole North-South division, irrational anti-Communism that feeds the whole complex—all this begot sharp response. From my former position as a well-loved Jesuit rector, "safe" in outlook, I became known as radical, leftist, somewhat one-sided, even far out in emphasis and, among the local "Birchers," a Communist. Incredibly one day I found a fifteen-foot banner flying from my homeroom window proclaiming "Marquette students for justice are Communists." One senior told his mother, "Mom, my classmates are calling me a Communist." Small wonder for a school that went solidly for Goldwater in `64 and even more solidly for Reagan in `80. Yet we continued to teach social justice and with a growing number of fellow faculty built awareness and a constituency for justice.

Dorothy Day's words came to mean much to me:

> What we do is very little, but it is like the little boy with a few loaves and fishes. Christ took the little and increased it. He will do the rest. What we do is so little we may seem to be constantly failing. But so did he fail. He met with apparent failure on the cross. But unless the seed fall into the earth and die, there is no harvest. And why must we see results? Our work is to sow. Another generation will be reaping the harvest.

The years beyond the Guatemala experience were roller coaster years: of joy and of frustration, of disillusionment with our country and our Jesuit province, and of admiration for so many individuals who could only be called outstanding.

I was buoyed by our Jesuit General Congregation in Rome in 1975 with its famous Decree Four which stated our identity and proclaimed our goal as a religious order to be the promotion of faith and justice and by its decree on poverty and solidarity with the poor. But then I was discouraged by the eight years that followed when our local leadership did next to nothing to implement the justice thrust. Whether it was fear of offending the people we served and depended on, or ignorance of how to proceed, or fear of alienating Jesuits in the ranks, little effective leadership was exercised, and the rich promise of the congregation was dashed.

I watched with sorrow as my beloved Indian towns in Guatemala were drenched with blood-tide of cruelty and death-squad extermination by Generals like Lucas Garcia and his successors. With dismay I watched as Reagan was elected in

1980, and the right-wing military and wealthy cheered the prospect of renewed military aid. In horror I saw Jesuit Rutilio Grande murdered, Jesuits in Guatemala and El Salvador slapped with death threats from the secret anti-Communist league, Archbishop Romero gunned down, his funeral sabotaged by gunfire, the four American women slaughtered by a death squad in El Salvador, the stream of refugees fleeing Indian towns for Chiapas and the United States. I watched my worst dreams materialize as the Committee for the Present Danger consolidated every major post in the State Department and in the Department for Defense and in arms-control negotiations, as the arms race raced to 1.6 trillion dollars while hunger and poverty were neglected.

Yet we cheered at the Peace movement, at the flow of information coming from Central America from groups like the Religious Task Force on Central America. We were exhilarated by the U.S. bishops' landmark pastoral letter on war and peace and on the arms race. And always there were the young I taught. Eager to know, concerned, wanting to make a difference, generous to join the *"lucha,"* the struggle for a better world. During these years many sections of the gospel opened up for me: Jesus as peasant became so much more real for me; his work of building a kingdom of justice and peace became so much clearer and yet so complex at the same time; the Cross and persecution and insult became the inevitable consequence for anyone truly concerned; and the contemplative springs of action became an absolute necessity for me. I thank God for this development, though it cost me very much.

## Depression

After flying home from the earthquake and Holy Week in San Lucas, a somewhat surprising development occurred in my life. Ordinarily, I'm optimistic and enthusiastic by temperament. Friends have kidded me about this for years. But a week after my return I found a clammy sadness clutching my gut. In short, I slid into a mild depression. In the morning I would wake up with this thick black cloud covering me like some garment. I could function as a teacher, but my happiness was smothered. I began to search for a cause and ruminated endlessly over my past life, replaying old atrocities and just sinking further into the mud. Then I'd junk it all and play a couple sets of competitive tennis and feel good for a while. But then back came the sadness and endless rumination.

Finally, I made an appointment with my good friend, Leo Graham, a clinical psychologist with whom I'd team-taught on the SSCA for years. Leo gave me a battery of psychological tests, listened patiently, and then smiled; "John, you've got a chronic low-level depression. Don't fight it, let it come; muck around in it for a while." He tracked its three triggering causes: first, the frustrations of my three years as a Jesuit superior. Second, the whole midlife crisis thing which I had been shelving: questions like "Is what I'm doing worthwhile? What have fifty-one years of life added up to? How will I spend the time left? What is my life for?" And third, the three Third World experiences which ripped the mask off the world's suffering and seared my very soul. A potent brew had been mixing for five years and was not being dealt with.

In my second appointment, Leo told me, "Basically you're healthy as a horse. It will pass. Face the reality of yourself; listen to your own emotional reactions, the pain and loneliness and frustration; don't repress it; cope with it realistically. Reroute your life a bit, get a change, do some retooling, work more with adults. Admit your limitations. You're tied into a huge problem that you can't change; you can only do what you can. Cultivate humor, and live a bit, and smile at the human situation; it's better to be a healthy jackass than a dead lion."

After this second appointment, I felt much better and so heartened that I stopped therapy. And the depression did lift, rays of light came, and zest for life returned slowly.

Yet that spring there was a strange concomitant feeling. All the time that I experienced depression, I felt in my inmost self a thirst and craving for God that came from deep within me. I felt that somehow or other there was much good here, that the depression was pushing my life onto a deep level, that the experience at Pope John's tomb was being strangely implemented.

It is so very hard to put my finger on all this. Since that spring, I found myself better able to speak more effectively to people suffering from depression and to console them and share their pain and give them hope. It's one of my life's beliefs that every suffering experience unites us with some segment of the human race and that the Lord will use it for the help of his people.

At the end of that school year, I was granted a sabbatical year and decided on the Jesuit School of Theology in Berkeley. Ready for some new experiences, I took off in mid-June for a favorite spot, St. Ignatius, Montana, a lovely Flathead Indian mission at the foot of 10,000-foot mountains in western Montana. From there, I hitchhiked some 2,000 miles through Glacier Park, Calgary, Banff, Lake Louise, Columbia Icefields, Jasper and Mt. Edith Cavell and Maligne Lake. I had a grand time hitchhiking, met marvelous people, laughed a lot, hiked all the mountains I could, photographed it all. Toward the end of August, I paused for a while at a parish near Mt. Rainier, where Jesuit friend Dan Weber and I almost did ourselves in climbing Pinnacle Peak, a thumb of rock with a 2,000-foot drop. With my new bifocals, tired but happy, in late September I settled in for my long-awaited sabbatical by the Golden Gate.

# 6

## Berkeley Sabbatical

My sabbatical, so eagerly awaited, was truly memorable. Difficult in many ways, but so worthwhile.

We lived in a place jokingly called Holy Hill, a consortium of seminaries clustered at the north end of the University of California Berkeley Campus in the Berkeley Hills overlooking the Bay and The City and Golden Gate bridge in the distance. In late September, forty men and women, mostly religious and priests, from Australia, France, Venezuela, Mexico, Canada, the Marshall and Caroline Islands and the United States, gathered for an opening eight-day retreat and then settled into a trimester year of course work as part of the Institute of Spirituality and Worship. Median age was thirty-nine I lived in a small community of three Jesuits in an apartment. We had a veritable smorgasbord of courses to choose from: the different offerings of the eight theological schools in the consortium, Catholic and Protestant, as well as courses at the University of California. At last I had a year to read widely in spirituality, scripture, developmental psychology and especially the great mystics.

Happily, it was not all study. Sunday mornings found me in a variety of places: over at San Quentin Federal Prison as chaplain, a sobering experience; up to the juvenile center in the hills above Oakland where teenagers in T-shirts color-coded according to their crimes prepped for San Quentin; in Marin County celebrating Mass for a marvelous group of families in a small worshiping community; and at the most famous Bay

Area liturgy in the Oakland Cathedral at 10:30.

Many Saturday afternoons, three theologians who served a nursing home in Pacifica would drop me off at the beach where I climbed the rocks and watched the great Pacific Ocean crash in, a sight I have never tired of. Memorable also were three prayer weekends at the Big Sur Camaldolese monastery, an aerie perched 1,500 feet above the ocean, where the hermits practiced complete solitude. For me it was a place that said "God Alone" and triggered a powerful desire to be alone with God and pray.

Daily I jogged across the upper campus, around the artificial track near the football stadium, through Telegraph Avenue with its street vendors and great book stores, and into Sproul Plaza where the human comedy was in play: Moonies, John Denver singers, the mime, Berkeley "babes" working in the dry fountain debunking the love ethics, "Save the Humpback Whale" crusaders, the black Oakland banjo player and dancers, the string quartet on the lower level, and a team of five characters, always vulgar, sometimes obscene, entertaining a few hundred students between classes. I can never remember a boring afternoon at Sproul Plaza. Cloud Cuckoo Land, and I loved it.

A highlight of the year was the companionship with young Jesuits in training, some of whom I had taught with at Marquette High or had counseled there, with Jesuit classmates now on the Jesuit School of Theology faculty and with the men and women in our program so talented and open and eager to learn. Our liturgies every Thursday morning so carefully prepared by a team of four with help from our liturgy director, Jake, featuring six very talented musicians were experiences of community and of God in our midst that I treasured. Little did I know how much I was to miss this rich liturgy in years to come.

In short, it was a year where God gifted me with so much. It wasn't easy being away from Milwaukee and without old friends, but it was rich and varied and deep.

# John of the Cross

One of the principal gifts of this sabbatical year was the superb course on the great Spanish mystic, John of the Cross, taught by Jesuit Fr. Mike Buckley, a born teacher, profound yet eloquent and moving. It was easily one of the most influential courses of my life, a source of nourishment to this very day.

Let me speak of what affected me so deeply during these days of grace. During our Jesuit philosophical studies, I had taken natural theology, the study of what we can know of God through reason by way of analogy, affirmation, and negation. In our theological studies we took hard courses on the one God and the Trinity which tried to pin God down in clear terms. But for John of the Cross it was so clearly opaque: God simply is the incomprehensible one, God is no thing, no limited essence, rather all in all, one who transcends our limited minds and explodes our categories. God cannot be grasped adequately by the human mind or pictured by our imagination. God is beyond all our concepts. He who is light in himself, supreme clarity, is darkness to the human mind. As the sun in itself is supreme light, yet too bright for the naked human eye to stare at directly, so God is to the human. Therefore, the more we know of God, the more we enter, not into clarity, but into naked mystery, darkness, into incomprehensibility. Faith then, as dark knowledge, with the Lord's word as guide, is the way we walk to him. Yet on every page, like a giant current, John has the incredible certitude of God's presence permeating creation and acting in the soul. This makes sense to me.

But this is not all. For this soaring mystic, God is first and foremost the Beloved, the Bridegroom who sues for the love of his bride: us. This is clear on almost every page of John's writings. His principle on spiritual direction is: in the first place, it should be known that if a person is seeking God, his beloved is seeking him much more. This incomprehensible one takes the first initiative, he is the hunter, the Hound of Heaven who pursues us out of love. He longs to take his own inner riches and pour his whole self into our created capacities for him, into bottomless caverns of our intellect and will and memory, faculties made for him.

John views heaven as the great wedding feast where God's love for me is consummated forever in ecstasy. We are *made* for this ecstasy, a forever gift of God to us, his beloved. And so death for John of the Cross is to move organically into the vision of God into eternal life. At the pinnacle of the mystical experience, John simply asks, "Tear aside the last veil that holds me back from you."

What struck me forcibly is the divine indwelling of the Trinity as the foundation of our spiritual lives; experiential awareness of that presence is the heart of the inner life. John urges us in his maxims: "Enter into yourself, and live and work in the presence of your Beloved who is very present loving you." "For your self is his dwelling and his secret chamber and hiding place; you are the temple of God. What more can you want?"

For years I'd looked at shining mountains like Ranier, Hood, St. Helen's, and the peaks of Glacier Park and then set out laboriously to climb them. Some of the most memorable days of my life have been spent climbing beyond forest and mountain meadow, onto rock and snow, through cloud layers to shining heights. John's analogy in the *Ascent of Mt. Carmel* is the journey to the top of the shining mountain of God. For him, the whole purpose of our years is to be captivated by this vision of the heights, to set out on the trail, to achieve the very summit, to begin here and now a love relationship with this great Beloved, to grow all the years of our life in love and union with God, to make that the great quest of our lives, to be open and let God's love take over in us and then to love all things in God. This journey to the summit truly begins when God touches the human person with his presence and awakens us with religious experience inviting us to the heights. Consolation without previous cause is that first step of all movements towards God. So it was for me.

A key insight of John's is that the central condition on which all hangs is purity of heart. As we climb this mountain towards union with God, we must have a single-minded search for God in the *whole* of our life, not just in compartments of it. This quest demands a detachment from all that is not God, a gradual purifying of my love till I love him alone and all things only in him. Some of this purification, especially of sense and sense appetites, I can do by myself with God's ordinary grace. But the deep purification of my radical selfishness and self-seeking is best done by God in his own way, the night of sense and spirit.

Here is a pertinent passage from Mike Buckley's lecture: "The heart of John of the Cross is this cryptic formula: Nothing together with God, only *in* God; God is not to be one of the many things you love, not #7 or #13 or #24 on the list of things you love, but he is to be the first. Loving something together with God makes light of him. The movement in all spirituality is beyond the pain-pleasure principle to loving God in himself, in nakedness of spirit." So John's favorite gospel quote: "Unless you renounce all ...; no man can serve two masters." John's analogy is the bird, bound either by a thread or by a cord and so unable to fly. Flat out, John will say, `God does not fit into an occupied heart.'"

Humanly, John will add from his own experience: "Now I ask you Lord, do not abandon me at any time, for I am a squanderer of my soul." And this resonates with so many of us. We are attracted to climb to the summit of the mountain but long to stay in the lush mountain meadows where limpid streams run and flowers bloom and the climate is mild. Here so many of us stagnate. We feel our own emptiness and restlessness, those deep caverns of feeling within us that ache for God. Yet we fill our days with rushing around, endless activity, distractions and pleasures, trying to fill the void. But it is hopeless. This Beloved urges us to tune into our depths, to know our capacity for God, to identify with it and to head for the heights. Purity of heart is our watchword, pulling free of all that holds us back, as we move up out of pleasant valleys and meadows of sense, up on the rocky heights onto the snowfields where the night of the spirit awaits.

The basic process here is to move beyond everything, even religious experience, to dark knowledge, to faith in God alone, to finally allow faith to call the shots: a conversion from knowledge of reason to faith as one's sure guide. The night of the spirit is to lead me to naked faith. You are my God. Nothing else is you. You are the ultimate support of my life. You ask a wholesale surrender in which the final purification of the soul takes place. John would have us know that the sufferings of this dark night is the dark side of God's grace, the shadow of his caressing hand. The depth of that suffering is a clear indication of the depth of the union to which God is calling the soul after these dark nights.

This night of the spirit is stiff stuff to read, but intelligible only when we realize that John is a mountain climber standing in the glory of the summit, surveying the trail below. What he says makes sense only in terms of that view and the attraction God gives to the heights.

Two images that John uses make much sense. He describes us as a piece of raw iron filled with impurities, thrust into a fire. The iron heats and glows, and then the metal impurities melt and flow away gradually till only pure iron is left, glowing with the fire, transformed by the fire until one with that fire. So is our transformation in God.

Or the process is like a window streaked with dirt and grease. We wash and rub and wipe until all the sunlight passes through so that we cannot see the glass itself so perfectly it transmits the light.

## Paul Tillich

Several other experiences stand out as well. In the course on the Ignatian Exercises, a definite grace for me was contact with Paul Tillich's marvelous article on sin and acceptance. Tillich treated sin, not as an act but more as a state of alienation or separation from ourselves, from others, from our society, and radically from God. One sentence that still sings out to me and resonates with my experience at Pope John's tomb is:

> We are separated from the mystery, the depth, the greatness of our existence. We hear the voice of that depth, but our ears are closed. *We feel that something radical, total and unconditional is demanded of us. And yet we don't know how to respond to bridge that separation.* And so we are separated yet found, estranged and yet belonging.

Yes, this is the reality of all of us, the bottom line of the human condition. Into this reality God comes and—surprise of surprises—he accepts us as we are. Faith, then, for Tillich is the courage to accept acceptance by the surprising God. This makes eminent sense to me and resonates in my soul. The marvel is that he accepts me as I am, with all my brokenness and loves me. He calls me to himself as his chosen one. He sends me out on his work as his instrument.

## Max Pearse

If you're lucky in life, you happen upon a few outstanding people whom you come to realize are great gifts of God to you. During my year at Berkeley I was gifted with a number of excellent teachers and treasured friends. Of all these, however, one stands clear, my blind saint, Max Pearse. Max was an Anglican priest in his fifties, in residence at the Episcopalian School of Theology. He was very well read in spirituality of the East and West and possessed a keen retentive memory and an infectious enthusiasm for life and people and a buoyant optimism. As a youth, he had been an avid mountain climber and rafter of the rivers of the West. After completing his studies, he volunteered for missionary work in Africa, which he loved. It was there that a bad case of diabetes came on him and progressively robbed him of his sight. He returned to the U.S. and began conducting seminars for theology students at Berkeley. Three of our ISW crowd heard of him and lined up a reading course on Teresa of Avila. They were much taken with his warmth, his perception, and his joyous affirmation of life. So I sought out Max for what I thought was to be a reading course on various loose ends for my last semester at Berkeley.

I found a thin, wiry, white-haired gentleman, nervous, quick in movement, tapping his way through life with a white cane. Surprisingly, after our first session, he took me to lunch at a nearby Turkish restaurant where we set up details of the course.

After several sessions, with unerring insight, Max spotted

that what I wanted to do was to digest all the currents of my life so far and fuse it into a synthesis of my spirituality at age fifty-two. "John, what you want to do is to write. Do it, for God's sake. Do it!" Something in me snapped into place. Of course, this was it. And so for the next two months I sat in my room and wrote some sixty pages to the strains of Mahler's "Resurrection Symphony." I found it nourishing and utterly absorbing.

Each week, after initial confusion, assembling of materials, and gestation, suddenly the diverse elements would snap into place and I could write, the words flowing intensely from the heart. Each Friday I brought ten or so pages of completed text to Max. He would say, "Now, John, read me your best." Unerringly, week after week, he went to the heart of what I was saying, picked the key insight, commented on it, questioned it, affirmed it, modified it, and then amplified it with memorable quotations that have become a part of my life. Over the weeks that followed, I saw this fragile, blind man as a beacon of light. For one who could not see, his inner vision was bright and penetrating. To this day, when I think of him, I think of a luminous human face suffused with light. I came to revere him as an authentic saint, one close to God. Our times together became more and more precious.

Max directed me into that great Hindu classic, *The Bhagavad Gita.* Through Max, I came to the great Swedish secular saint, Dag Hammarskjold, and his classic *Markings* became one of my enduring favorites. He introduced me for the first time to the French mystic, Simone Weil; her *Waiting for God*, a record of God's invasion of her life, grew to be a continuing inspiration in the years to come.

Max's comments and his favorite quotes, repeated till they dawned on me, were rich sources of insight and further reflection. Here follow a set of his quotes: some are original, some are from *Markings* or *Waiting for God*; but all are personally appropriated by him and given as gift to me. I've tried to arrange them under a few general headings.

*His affirmation of life and of one's past history:*

"Thanks, God, for that which has come already; usually it's more than I can celebrate in a lifetime."

"For all that has been, thanks; for all that will be, yes."

"All suffering you undergo unites you with some new segment of the human race."

And the quote he loved to repeat till it came home to me in all its force: "Everything is designed to bring you home, if only you could work with it."

When a blind man who lives not in bitterness but in radiant joy tells you this, you take notice.

*Comments on mid-life which stuck deeply with me:*

"Midlife means coming to terms with our limits; our boundaries locate us and define us; they tell us who we are and who we aren't. Accept those limits and laugh at them."

"Midlife is that time when one decides what is food and what is bones to be left; less vitality, yes, but more discrimination."

"As you get older, what holds you is the authenticity."

"Everyone has a story he is meant to live out."

"As for the past, let the dead bury their dead; but for you, come follow me."

*God and the Inner Life:*

"Faith is the marriage of God and the soul."

"The lovers of God have no religion but God alone."

"Thou whom I do not know but whose I am."

"Not I, but God in me."

"The East tells us clearly: if the whole world is an illusion, then only a fool gets caught in it. The inner world is most important, so live in it."

"We carry within us the wonders we seek outside us."

"The best, most wonderful thing that can happen in this life is that you should be silent and let God work and speak."

*Giftedness:*

"Yes, have sense of your own giftedness; but your special giftedness, John, is youngness in heart, an optimism and enthusiasm of soul to see the kernel of truth under the grubby husk, to spot the spark of divinity and the desire for God in a person, and to invite that person to depth. Optimism in our despairing age will increasingly be at a premium. What we must do is give people some glimmer of hope."

# 7

## The Difficult Years, 1977 - 1980

### Purification

In the fall of 1977, I settled down again in the apostolate of my
choice at Marquette High, eager to implement the vision and
ideals acquired at Berkeley. As co-department head of theology, a member of the pastoral team, organizer of the adult
theology program and retreat director for parents' retreats, I
felt I had a unique opportunity to promote the "Faith that does
justice." The adjustment back into the limited high school
world proved to be much more difficult than I had imagined.
Though I was very happy to be back with young people again,
I truly missed the Berkeley group, the intellectual stimulation,
and the luxury of leisure to read and reflect.

A small group of us worked very hard during the next five
years to establish an integral global-awareness and justice
thrust into our courses and into the school. But increasingly we
found ourselves wrestling with frustration and anger over the
slow pace of change in our province, in our Jesuit community,
and in our school milieu. Our official rhetoric in General
Congregation 32 and in the Jesuit Secondary Educational Asso-
ciation was very clear, yet our corporate response was so slow,
so tentative, so cautious. I found these years quite difficult.

On my two annual retreats directed by Joe Diamond, S.J.,
a wise director of priests from Maryland, I wrestled with my
demons and tried to come to some basic poise that would not

betray my ideals. Patiently Joe worked with me. His favorite refrain was: "As you travel on through life, my brother, whatever be your goal, keep your eye upon the donut and not upon the hole." Instead of concentrating on the result of my work, the successes or failures we experienced, he insisted that all we could do is to plant seeds in the young, to nourish those seeds, and to leave results to God. To my rising frustration he would have me face Jesus who said; "Peace, John. My peace I give you. I do love you and always will. I send you out on my work. Receive the Spirit; it is a work of forgiveness and reconciliation. Remember: peace in your heart."

Again and again, Joe reminded me it was God's work, not mine. God is the Potter molding my flawed clay, the Tapestry Maker working in the story of my life, asking me only to go his way and do his will.

In all this I was growing in consciousness that what was going on was a stripping away of narcissism, of self-conceit, of the success syndrome, of my own willfulness, of my sense of self-importance. And it wasn't I doing this but life experience doing it. A passive purification of sense and spirit, a growth. The cross of Christ is truly the solid way.

Yet along with this painful set of realizations was a growing desire for God. One night on retreat, I walked out under the sky and stared at the stars. It came home to me that the infinite God is what I'm made for, God alone, to be with and in this Person. Simply speaking, I'm made for ecstatic union with him. How many years of life do I have? Ten, twenty years, who knows? And then life with Him, forever.

All else, then, is relative, a heap of straw. Yes, God is what I'm all about. I'm pointed like an arrow to him. This God knows me in all my particularities, and he alone loves me infinitely without measure. This same God has moved into my life, claimed me in a Providence that works through hundreds of details and chance occurrences and my own free-will actions and decisions and failures and faults and sins. He is the Potter, the Tapestry Maker declaring himself steadily in the story of my soul, intervening in my history to put me where I am today. It's for me then to say yes to him inviting and purifying me, to do his will day by day. And so that night I said yes to my history;

I'll go on till the Lord calls me home. I am where I should be, so let me bloom at MUHS where I am planted. Let me sow seed and plant in gentleness of spirit but leave results to the Lord.

But these four years were not easy ones. Slowly, I let go of my own plans and projects and success. I passed the torch to younger leadership and turned more and more to God. This was a painful process; in fact, closure was only complete in 1985—it would take that long. Yet along with constant struggle, there were moments that stood out where God struck into my life strongly.

## CLC Groups

For years, ever since my scholastic days at St. Louis University High School, I had moderated sodality or Christian Life Community groups of young people. Typically, several outstanding young people who have a thirst for God and want to serve others in some significant way will come to me in their sophomore or junior year and ask: "Father, I want to come closer to God; could we build a small Christian community where I could share my thoughts and feelings and faith with other guys my own age." This is a marvelous request, and it touches me deeply. There is no way I can refuse. So we form a Christian sharing group of eight to ten young people and begin to meet evenings from 7:00 to 10:00 every week or every other week. I insist with the lads that each meeting always climax with the Eucharist as central to the group's life. These simple, touching, full-participation Masses, where young people can share reflections and speak their hearts out to God openly in prayer, have been for me a constant experience of God, some of the most precious moments of my life.

I remember so well one such Mass with an outstanding group of lively juniors at the end of a four-day closed retreat in a lovely A-frame house on Lake Michigan's shore. These ten lads had taken to shared prayer like birds to the air. At our last Mass on Saturday night, I suggested that we have a simple ceremony where we prayed over each other silently for the deeper gift of the Holy Spirit and for whatever the person needed. And so, after giving each lad the Body and Blood of the Lord, with the whole group sitting in a circle on the floor, a flickering candle in the middle, "Amazing Grace" as background music, I got up and imposed my hands on the head of Shazzie Sherer and prayed silently for this special lad, then spoke a word to him telling him simply how much the Lord loved him and wanted him as close friend. I moved to Jack Wisnewski and so on. A simple touching ceremony that triggered deep prayer in me as I prayed for these special young people whom I had come to esteem and love. The boys did the same, praying over each other. When they came, one by one, to pray over me, their prayer pulled waves of strong prayer out of my depths. Their simple words swept me away: "When you came into my life, God came into my life. What I am with God today, I owe to you. You stuck with me and believed in me, even when I failed. You have been a true father for me. I love you."

We returned home and plunged into a hectic week of class and activities. I was drained. And then a most remarkable thing happened. In the four or five days that followed, whenever I turned from teaching to some quiet time, to walk outside after school or a visit to chapel, it was as though a hidden spring somewhere deep inside me suddenly burst open and my spirit began to rise and sing within me. A tide of joy rose along with an attraction to God who dwelt in my depths. Instant prayer and contact with God was mine for those days following that retreat. I marveled at this and then mentioned it to each lad; his experience was identical to mine. It was then that I realized our prayer to the Holy Spirit that night had been answered.

## 1978: Prairie Mountain Mass

On my return from Berkeley, I found a real delight. Three groups of outstanding young people soon had me lined up for CLC groups. In 1978, at a closed freshmen retreat, I met a most impressive young man, Peter Carter, a lad who loved the outdoors and maneuvered me into two camping trips that summer. Peter was a true delight: a regular guy who loved the wilderness and swimming in waterfalls, he was sensitive to the feelings of others, warm and caring, gifted with an ardor of faith. During his sophomore year we discussed forming a CLC group, with him as organizer. That summer I was to be assistant pastor on the Flathead Indian reservation in St. Ignatius, Montana, a lovely town of 900 in the Mission Valley nestled at the foot of the lofty 10,000-foot, forested Mission Range of mountains. I invited Peter to climb Glacier Park with me; to my surprise he accepted.

And so on a warm day I will always remember, we drove into Glacier Park, got out on the trail around 9:00 A.M. toward Grinnel Glacier shimmering in the distance high up on the Divide. We skirted Swiftcurrent Lake, climbed steadily above huge Josephine Lake and then higher and higher till our trail dropped sharply 2,000 feet to the powder blue waters of little Grinnell Lake. On the left a waterfall roared down a cliff, ahead lay the largest glacier in the Park, and above it Salamander Glacier, plastered against the wall of the Divide.

That night, tired from the trail, we drove south to Browning, Montana, through open range country looking for a scenic place to have Mass together. Twenty miles south of town we turned onto a dirt road and drove to the top of a hill facing the mountains. There at sunset I spread my Guatemalan blanket facing west to the snow-clad peaks. We then celebrated one of the most memorable Eucharists of our lives.

The day had been splendid, climbing the shining mountains to the source of the streams. Peter picked a special gospel reading and spoke on it. There in the middle of the vast open prairie the Lord came to us in His Body and Blood. Once again I raised the perfect gift from humankind to the Father. I gave Peter the Body and Blood of the Lord and then wandered off for fifteen minutes to walk the boundless prairie in the descending twilight. As I walked, I became conscious of the night breeze blowing free over the prairie from the distant peaks. Wild night birds danced across the sky, their cries echoing over the rolling hills. Above, the stars wheeled in silent glory. I walked in all that glory with the sacramental Christ in my heart. I was caught up with the fullness of it all, with the very ecstasy of nature; joy and gratitude filled my heart. I felt all around me the enormous play of God in His creation. All this, mountain and cataract, prairie and stars and wild birds for me, for us.

Heart full, I returned to the flickering candle where Peter and I shared prayer. Young Peter spoke out to God so ardently in thanks and praise for the glory of the night. It was moving and deep. I gave Peter my blessing. We told each other that we would never forget this splendid evening, the Lord's climax to a stunning day. O Holy Night.


## Nancy

One person I'll always remember from those years was Nancy, in her early forties, married and mother of four, a high-spirited skier. I met her at a cabin Mass I had for some forty people in the Porcupine Mountains at Christmas time. At that Mass and the party afterward we celebrated her victory over cancer. After treatment, her symptoms had gone, and she was free of melanoma. We had a good talk that night. Later on the next winter I got a call from her husband, Paul, a dentist. Nancy had been stricken again and was in the hospital. It was terminal. Remembering the cabin Mass and our talk, she asked to see me. I found Nancy weak and in great pain. She looked at death with level eyes. For this young woman who loved to fly down the mountainside, life had now narrowed to a hospital bed and four white walls.

Nancy wanted to talk about dying. No nonsense or wasted words, she spoke of her feelings of uselessness. She who had done so much for family and friends—what was she anymore to husband or kids or friends?

I listened and then spoke simply of the Guatemalan Indians and what they taught me of death. Their realism was essentially this: Grandpa's job in life was to grow corn; for the Mayan this is truly a religious rite. Grandpa did the job God gave him and did it well. And now, lying on a mat in his *casa*, sick unto death, Grandpa is doing the last job God gives him, the job of suffering and dying, and he's doing it well. And so his family went about life in the *casa*: cooking tortillas and chatting and eating and living as Grandpa lay dying. So matter of fact, so real in their attitude.

So I told her: "Nancy, the one chore all of us have is to do what God gives us to do. For years you've done the job he gave you: to be wife to Paul and a mother to these kids, and you've done it well. Now God is giving you one last job, one final chore, to suffer and die, to do it well, to say yes to life and to the Lord of life, to say yes to your progressive diminishment and to find God in it all."

Such easy words for a healthy me to say, but they came from some deep part of me and touched her soul. Later, Paul and her friends told me how much those words meant to her. Then Nancy told me how she coped with her pain. Level-eyed and unemotional, she told me very simply that when the pain got bad, she and Paul prayed to God for one favor: "Lord, make your presence felt sensibly. Let me know you are with me now." Whenever she asked for that grace, God gave her that sense of himself and his presence. With great simplicity, she told me that was the way she was making it through cancer until the end.

We talked for an hour: she told me how much our talks meant, how I somehow stood for God in her life, how she felt God had come through me. I felt humbled and awed, stirred deeply, inspired by this lovely woman of faith, close to this God who moves and touches the human heart in such striking ways. On March 5, we celebrated Nancy's Mass of Christian Burial.

## Summer 1980: Molokai and Fr. Damien

A sudden gift. In early July, I found myself on a 747 winging to Honolulu to help as an assistant pastor in a Maryknoll parish for four weeks. The parish, ten minutes from Waikiki, was mostly Chinese people. I thoroughly enjoyed working with them. On days off, I traveled all over Oahu and swam at every good Pacific beach I could find. Friends there urged me to see the other islands, and I puzzled over which to see. But after a visit to the Sacred Heart Fathers' museum and shrine to the memory of Fr. Damien of Molokai, the choice seemed clear.

A word of background. In my sophomore year at Campion, I had read the life of the famous leper priest, Damien. He became one of my life heroes. Over the years I read every book on Damien I could find. Through the Sacred Heart Fathers, I found out that one of their priests, Fr. Fernandez, was resident chaplain of the leper settlement and would welcome me and put me up in his rectory. So, toward the end of July, I flew in a small plane along the rugged Pali cliffs on the north coast of Molokai to a small airstrip. There Fr. Fernandez met me, and he and a leper took me on a tour of the once inaccessible triangle of land three miles in breadth and length, where lepers were left to die.

That afternoon and evening I met the lepers in the hospital and surrounding compound around Kalaupapa, the modern leper settlement. I shook hands with John, a gregarious man without fingers on his right hand and with artificial legs. He joked, "I've got no problems with mosquito bites on my ankle." I had a marvelous chat with a lovely little old lady in the hospital. Leprosy had taken her sight, but she had a glorious smile and an inner radiance. In her hands she fingered a rosary. She told me, "I can no longer see or do much, so I just pray to God all day long." When I asked her about her sickness, she said with a luminous smile, "We mustn't grumble at what the good Lord sends us." I felt cheap before her simple faith. Her words were one more call to me to live a life more in touch with the Lord who loves me and wants to lead me to far greater depth.

Each of the three days that followed I headed out in the morning in Father's battered car, drove the cow paths three miles to the original site of Damien's labors and spent the day reading parts of his life and reflecting on them. Nothing much remains there, except the little church where Damien cele-brated Mass each morning, the graveyard, and some markers of the settlement buildings. I went into the church and sat there, looking at the holes cut in the floor for the lepers to spit into, at the little altar where this hero celebrated Eucharist, and at the communion railing where he spoke to his lepers. I remember reflecting on his call so well articulated by Adlyth Moriss' marvelous TV documentary, "Damien."

They must have one priest who belongs to them, to prove to them that God has not forgotten them; I want to be their priest. I beg to stay on at Molokai. You see, a man enters the religious life in answer to a call. Later, if he is lucky, he receives a call within a call. He finds the niche that he was meant to fill. This is my niche, this is what I was meant to do, this is why I was born.

Over and over again, I read Fr. Damien's vivid account of his coming to Molokai and of his first Eucharist in this church.

The little church starts filling up with, God forgive me, creatures from the nightmare, limping, shuffling, coughing, spitting, touching with the fingers they have left the rosaries hung around their necks. They keep on coming till the church is filled up to the railing. They crowd the window sills, the doorways, they fill the church to overflowing, not only with their corrupting bodies, not only with the stench, but with a sadness so unbearable I stand dumb in my vestments. The vomit rises in my throat. I choke it back. They kneel and wait, and finally in a voice I have never heard before, I say the words: In the name of the Father and of the Son and of the Holy Spirit.

I replayed in my imagination that famous scene twelve years after that day, at this very communion rail when he told his people that he was in truth a leper.

My dear children, I have called you here to tell you something that concerns us all. From the day I came to live among you I have always said 'we lepers' because I wanted to be one of you. God has seen fit to grant my wish. Now I can never leave you. For I am in truth a leper. Receive me, rejoice with me and remember always: whatever happens, God knows best.

Then I would walk out north of the church along the great lava cliffs that poked their huge fingers into the surf crashing endlessly in spray. I saw the spot where Damien, unable to go to confession because his provincial was not allowed to land on Kalawao for fear of contagion, rowed his little boat out to the ship moored off shore and shouted his humble confession of sins above the noise of the surf to his provincial on deck above. I'd wander back and look at the tombstone of this "martyr of charity": then I'd move to the tombstone of his lay helper, Joe Dutton, a man of steel and great heart; and then to the grave of Sister Marianne. For three days I walked where heroes lived and walked. I would always end in his deserted church and listen to Damien. I guess I loved this man because he was so human. An impulsive Belgian farm boy, with no finesse, passionately devoted to his suffering people, yet angry and upset at official agencies who wanted to dump the lepers there and forget them, one whose impulsiveness often betrayed him, a saint with warts, a hero with obvious flaws, a man who questioned himself, yet one who found Christ in the poor and sick and experienced him there as I had in Guatemala.

Listen to Damien as he reviews his life:

> Did I do more harm than good? Did I betray you, Lord? Was I a defective priest? Was I stubbornly following the bent of my own temperament? But it was my temperament to seek you with a passion that consumed me. Once I had felt the wound of love there was no other way. You were with me in the lepers' shacks. You let me hear a festering mass of flesh still praise your name. The agonies I consoled, the wounds I nursed were yours: the agony and the wounds of Christ. Tell me this is true, Lord. Tell me this is true. One word and all these doubts will vanish like smoke before the wind. If it is these doubts that come between us Lord, then I will cast them out. In your name, Lord, I cast them out. Whatever I have done for good or ill, I am your priest. You are my God. I trust your prodigious love.

## An October Bike Ride—A Turning Point

It's a lovely Saturday afternoon in October. I hop on my bike and do a leisurely twenty-two-mile ride through the fall foliage: Wisconsin in all its glory. All of a sudden a river of joy and peace and happiness rises in me and flows on and on as I bike. Many positive thoughts occupy me on this lyrical day. The words of Isaiah 43 come through strongly, words I have reflected on in recent retreats: "Do not cling to the events of the past and dwell on what happened long ago. Watch for the new thing I am about to do. It's happening already. You can see it now."

I reflect on the fact that my fifty-sixth year will soon be beginning. It's time to say, "I spent years and years here at Marquette High building up youth retreats, Christian Life Community groups, counseling, the theology program, summers with the Summer School of Catholic Action, theological renewal through summer courses, then taking on the superior's job serving this community and leading them into renewal. Then the years as theology department head, the summers in the Third World and that whole global awareness project, the efforts to bring that awareness and the thrust for structural justice and peace more into my school, new courses and programs pioneered, Bread for the World, more retreats and more CLC groups: twenty-two years of hard work and it has been good and much good has been done. And so to say yes to it all and thank God for the good."

But now I'm almost fifty-five . My contribution has been largely made. It's time to let go, to turn things over to a younger generation of Jesuits and lay teachers; they have the energy and enthusiasm to run all these projects and make their unique contribution. Let the new generation do it. As for myself, drop compulsion and sense of obligation and feel a sense of freedom growing. The years of pouring out my energies are over. It's time to move to a more mellow, graceful, harmonious level; to let the restless, compulsive desires die; to enjoy the richness of life, to experience space and breadth and allow contemplation and wisdom grow. Finally, to drop all the oughts and shoulds, to accept the now that the Lord gives me, to enjoy it, to delight in the present, to rejoice in all the good things I have, to glory in this lovely fall day, in the marvelous people God puts on my path, to touch what people I can with what talents I have and to help bring them to the Lord from where they are. Age fifty-

# 8

## Summer of 1981

### Twenty-five Years a Priest

It's May 1981, and Peter and Bill and Mike and Dan and the rest of my senior CLC group are on a prayer retreat at the big A-frame cabin fronting on a Lake Michigan beach. The first night of the retreat I spread out on the floor ten slips of paper with selected Scripture quotes on God and his love and care for us. There by candlelight each of us picks his own slip, reads it silently and then out loud to the group, comments on its significance. When I look at my slip I am amazed. For the second year in the row my text is Isaiah 41.

> You have been chosen, my friend,
> I will never let you go.
> Fear not, I am with you;
> I am your God.
> I will strengthen you and help you.

I read these lines to my lads and then try to explain how these words have such special meaning for me: "You, I have chosen as my friend. You, twenty-five years ago I ordained as my priest. You some forty-one years ago, as a little freshman, I chose and called you to be my own. Never will I let you go. I am God. I am with you." I try to tell these lads what this means to me, but words fail, so for the next two days of this retreat I walk the sands of the Michigan shore, stare out over the waves, and turn over and over in my mind the love and care and personal choice of my God, feeling his presence and strength with me. Isaiah's quote goes on my desk top where I see it every day.

Fine celebrations follow. Fr. John Bernbrock and I celebrate our twenty-fifth with a student Mass and then a marvelous Mass for our parents and friends in the school gym. Some 400 parents and former students come, as John and I share the Mass and each speaks a few words at homily time. I try to put together my thoughts on these years of priesthood and what I want to say to these people for whom I have worked and come to know and love over the years.

There's a marvelous line in Alan Paton's book *Cry, The Beloved Country* that comes back to me again and again when I think about priesthood. When someone tries to thank the old black preacher for his kindness and tells him, 'You are a good man,' the old man says simply: 'No, I'm just a weak and sinful man, but the Lord has laid his hands on me, and that is all.'

To me that says it exactly. The Lord has laid his hands on me, and that is all. In April 1940 when I was a freshman at Campion, 100 pounds dripping wet, in the first closed retreat of my life, unexpectedly God broke through to me personally and touched my life deeply. I can remember the day clearly. A great first grace in which was contained everything, the start of it all; from that spring on, it has always been a settled, axiomatic thing that I would be a Jesuit and a priest. This to me is the gift of God, and that is mystery!

I have no clue as to why me, no clue other than God's mysterious love and that mystery only grows through the years. I've watched priests leave, classmates, fine men; I've watched young people wrestle with this vocation and commitment finding it so difficult to decide, and I say "Why has it been so clear for me over the years?" All I can say is, "This is gift." God has somehow or other laid his hands on me, has continually over the years done it, and that is all. I thank God for His gift. I'll never understand it.

### "You, alone."

It's now the end of May, 1981. This year I choose to make my annual eight-day retreat at Notre Dame of the Lake, a sprawling complex of buildings north of the city, built on a cliff overlooking Lake Michigan. I decided that spring to choose a woman, Sr. Lorraine Aspenleiter, to be my retreat director.

The first night of the retreat I took a long walk on the cliff high above Lake Michigan, listening to the crash of the surf and the sound of the gulls and looking down the long shoreline. After all the rush of student retreats, celebrations, exams, grades and graduation, it was so blessed to just walk in the peace of twilight, to capture some sense of my deeper self again and to sense God's presence all about me. I mulled over the text Lorraine had given me. I heard John the Baptist at the Jordan ford tell me, "That's the one, go on, follow him." We walked behind this Jesus till he turned, looked at us and spoke, "What are you looking for?" What do you want?" And my only answer to that could be, "You, Lord, You; nothing else really satisfies any more; where do you stay?" His simple answer was: "Come and see, John." My answer, "You, Lord, You," came from the very core of me and I knew it. Yes, for eight days I was to come and see and dwell with him. I was so glad to be there, walking out into the night, expectant as I began this important retreat.

At our next conference I told Lorraine of the puzzling reality I was experiencing. Really two levels of prayer were going on. I would get up early in the morning, set aside an hour of prayer for the Lord, sit down to pray, and so often it was words, words, a jumble of things hustling for my attention; my mind would wander horribly. After a period like this I'd say, "What a complete bust my prayer life is. What am I doing? Am I really interested in God or am I fooling myself?"

And yet there was another level going on, the experiential. I would go bike riding in the afternoon and look and see spring coming, clouds passing overhead, streams glistening in the afternoon sun, and my whole person would be caught up in joy and in the sense of God pervading his whole creation, and I would sing and praise him. I would lie in bed for awhile after my alarm sounded, and my mind would be completely clear; awareness of myself and God with me would be there, desire for God would rise up clean and strong and unencumbered from my depths. I would look at the young people and their fragility and their rich potentiality as I counseled them and taught them and sensed God in them. Reading the divine office in the morning or the *Confessions of St. Augustine* or *Markings,* I'd find sentences would jump off the page and put me in living contact with the Lord. Eucharist, bringing the Lord to a class or a parish or to a CLC group at night, was an experience of the Lord for me. Visiting Nancy in the hospital, walking amid apple trees in springtime, watching a jet soar up into the sunset sky, cross-country skiing in new snow, these and many more, in the middle of my day, were living contacts with the Lord, not unusual events, but frequent occurrences. The words of Romans 8:26 came home to me: We really don't know how to pray. The Spirit prays in us, creating the deep desires of the human heart, desires and impulses far too deep for words. Only the Spirit knows what this is all about.

I felt on an experiential level that a real centering was taking place in me. But when I set aside a long prayer period to speak to God, my speaking seemed shallow, words only, making speeches, and these amid endless distraction. A bust! I told Lorraine how puzzling all this was, confusing. What was wrong?

Lorraine was clear and direct; she said, "You want prayer to be patterned, to come at special periods you schedule in, to be absorbing experiences, to be times filled with insight. Instead, what you are getting is deep desires way down inside you, God's touches in your life, your depths suddenly uncovered by life and tears of joy and awareness cut loose when you least expect it. John, this is God's way of dealing with you. Receive his touches graciously; let his action when it comes flow in you; let God take you his way. Let him do what he wants in you and with you. There is much more prayer going on than you think. Maybe your prayer period is really your biking, your walking in nature, your stumbling on phrases like Augustine's "Lord give me yourself" or the Office's "Lord you brought up the sun this day because you love us." Go with what God is doing within you, John. Trust him. Let your life be your prayer. Wait in peace for God in the midst of your life."

This for me was very freeing and affirming. On the second day, she posed a question that was to hound me. "John, we use so many words in our teaching and conversations, so many words come into daily life through magazines and papers and TV. Why not throw all these words out and for this day ask yourself one question and one only: What is my word? What is the one word I want to speak out to my God? When I think of my unique relationship with God what word or words well up in me? What is my word? Think that over this day and put it in just a few words, two or three at most." "Lorraine," I said, "that's impossible. How can I ever put fifty-five years of a relationship into two or three words?" She said, "Well, don't work at it. Just let it come."

So I pondered that for a day, curiously at peace. The next morning as I was climbing the big Lake Michigan bluff right before my conference with her, the word surfaced effortlessly in me. My word was simply this: "You alone, God; you alone." It just seemed to come out of my depths in silence and to rest there making complete sense. I remembered the day ten years before at Campion when I walked into Mass late and the simple phrase of the first song, "You Are My God," took my breath away and held me. I remembered the day when, laughing and joking, a crew of Jesuits drove to the Camaldolese Monastery perched high above the Pacific, and the place abruptly spoke out "God alone" and triggered an enormous desire for solitude to pray to this God. And now this—"You, alone"—as my unique word before God.

Yes, Lord, as other previous sources of happiness grow dead or don't any longer satisfy me, God alone. As human persons increasingly prove incapable of filling me and my desire for full intimacy, God alone. I looked down at the waves streaming onto the beach below, and what came to me was the biblical expression, "deep calls out to deep" in the roaring of the waves, a deep calling out to my deep, calling me to seek you, God alone, now finally after all these years. I was overwhelmed. There in the morning sunshine on the brow of the hill, I asked this God of the lake and infinite air to come to me, to attract me so deeply to himself, to capture my heart and make me a man of prayer, to let this radiate over my whole day so that I would live each day with my God.

I told this to Lorraine; she looked me in the eyes and said very simply and solemnly. "John, you have an authentic call to the very Person of God." I asked her to explain and she did. Somehow or other that simple statement resonated with my experience of ten years and voiced clearly what was there. From then on it was a focal statement for me. A giant foundation stone that simply stated my deepest identity, the inner reality of who I was, my authentic core, the way I was to follow and walk. I thank God for that statement, that affirmation.

Then she asked me to turn my concern to what holds me back from being myself before God and with God all day long? "What is it that blocks the authentic self in you? Ask God to reveal that to you."

For the next day again in peace I faced my own shallowness, my idealistic desires turned compulsive, my anger and frustration as passionate projects were blocked or criticized or opposed, my bitterness, the turmoil in me that obscured my true bent. I puzzled over the years of my life in the context of that simple question and asked God to reveal it to me more fully.

The next morning, the fourth day of the retreat, I went out after breakfast to pray my Office, and there in Psalm 37 was the grace of the retreat waiting for me. I read it once and was astounded. It seemed that each phrase had been written for me alone. It was as though God himself was speaking with infinite care directly to me, meeting me in the middle of my life.

> Commit to the Lord your way;
> Trust in him; he will act. Take delight in the
> Lord and he will grant your heart's desires....
> Give up your anger, forsake your wrath. Be not
> vexed; it will only bring you harm.

Each word was pregnant with meaning. "Commit." Turn

it over to the Lord, give it away for keeps, put it in his hands and let him call the shots. "Your Way." Your life journey, your whole history, the complex process you are involved in, especially since 1971. "To the Lord." You are in his hands; he is the great Potter, the great Tapestry Maker forming and molding you the way he wants. You are precious in his sight; he chose you; he will never let you go; you need never fear. So let him call the shots now. In this retreat, let him visit you and touch you when he wants, as much as he wants. As he always has anyhow in your past. Look at his surprises over the years. Why not go with it? Be the hitchhiker you are, "Lord, where are you going? Let me go with you." So relax, don't be nervous. It's all gift. Without his giving, you really can't do anything or take a step to him. Trust in him and he will act. That is his promise. Leave it to the Lord and wait for him.

"Delight in the Lord." Leave behind your compulsive patterns, your anger, your frustration. You've lost humor, a sense of joy and of delight; the ability to turn to him like a little child and to play before him, to awaken in wonder to all the beauty he put around you, to find him everywhere. To discover the Lord in the beauty of springtime, in summer rain, in the cloudy day, in sunlit morning, in a thousand colors of green, in a perfect dandelion, in long green grass and rolling in delight in it, in running free as the wind along the Lake Michigan cliff, in bicycling, in exercising your body and yoga and stretching muscles, in apple blossoms, in sunset and long shadows, in the young and the beauty of human beings, in the lake and its waves and swells, in swimming in cold water, in swallows diving and soaring, in joy in starlight and the night and the silent passage of clouds before the moon. To delight in each of these. God's gifts to you. To play before the Lord in wonder and joy as a free spontaneous child of fifty-five.

"He will grant all your desires." Wait patiently for the Lord to come and act. The best things are the things the Lord does himself. Expect the unexpected and be ready to go with it.

This passage in Psalm 37 is probably what the Lord has targeted for me on this retreat. I am amazed how it comes to me almost by chance as the first psalm of the morning office, how it jars my attention and how each word speaks to me so richly.

Over and over again I explore it and pray and write in my journal.

It triggers in me a wave of joy and delight and peace in which I swim for days. Prayer comes from my heart and flows easily to the Lord. The whole of nature becomes a living sacrament that breathes God, God, God, this God who cares for me and leads me and touches my life. The way in this retreat seems so clear to me: to be at peace with whatever God does within me. Yes, be quiet, be observant, be aware and delight in what you discover; just let it unfold. God is doing things his own way; go with it. I'm like a surfer who just caught a big wave and is riding in joy to the shore, or like a wing glider catching a thermal and soaring with the surge to the High Sierra.

Then suddenly a set of Scripture texts glow into life and nourish me. The Moses burning-bush event becomes my standard stance for prayer. I put myself before the Lord and hear the words from the tabernacle, "John, John." "Yes, Lord, here I am." "John, take off your shoes, you are on sacred ground, the ground of encounter with me; I am the God of the stars and the sea, the God of Abraham and Moses, of Isaiah, Jeremiah and Ezekiel, the God of David and Daniel, the God of John the Baptist and Mary and Paul, of Augustine and Francis and Thomas, of Ignatius, Teresa, and John of the Cross, of Damien and Teresa of Calcutta, of Helder da Camara and Archbishop Romero and Bishop Casaldaliga, of Merton and Berrigan, of Peter and Tom and Mike, and I am your God." So I'd take off my shoes and be with the Lord intent on his very person. A grand way to start.

The next day the morning prayer of the Church grabs me.

"O God, you are my God whom I seek; for you my flesh pines and my soul thirsts like desert earth, parched, life-less without water. My soul clings fast to you. In the shadow of your wings I shout for joy. You are my help, your right hand upholds me."

These lines strike to my very soul. I walk around alone in a small chapel saying them out loud with great meaning to the Lord present. As Pentecost nears, I read from the Divine Office:

John, if you love me, if you try to seek me and do my will, my Father will love you and we will come to you and take our abode, our permanent dwelling place within you. You will be a living breathing temple in which we dwell. We will send the Spirit, the counselor, the great wise friend, the consoler to lead you on your journey, to create in you desires which lie too deep for words.

Once more I stumble on this passage from the Psalms:

> For God alone
> My soul waits in silence,
> my hope is in him
> So be still, my soul,
> before the Lord
> and wait patiently for him.

I'm moved to go into bodily-position prayer, acting out in my body what I feel in my soul: bending before the Lord in adoration, lying face down on the ground before him as a begging sinner, needing everything, asking him to help me, heal me, inspire me; lying on my back spread-eagled, asking him to come to me, giving him my life, my power of loving, my deep desires.

The advantages of Notre Dame of the Lake is that there are four Blessed Sacrament chapels on the grounds: the big church where I go at night and can be alone with God and pray as I want and say words out loud to him and come close to the tabernacle and speak. I come to enjoy patient sitting before the Lord in chapel, letting what happens happen, not patterning anything. How utterly real, a truly good way of prayer, being my authentic self with him, completely spontaneous with him, God of my life.

I look back on the days of this retreat with wonder. I'm amazed at how all this has flowered and come to explicit awareness. I feel it as so true: "You have an authentic call to the very person of God. Follow it." God is so good to me these days; I feel like a person transformed, glowing within. And I know that it is his gift, a gift that calls me to deeper life in the years ahead.

In the last few days of this extraordinary retreat, Lorraine gave me a few pieces of advice I was to find very helpful. So many strong deep feelings rise over a period of weeks and months, feelings that clamor for expression, that cause difficulty: which to follow and which to leave behind? Lorraine encouraged me to subject them to questioning. "From what spirit does this flow? From my selfish side, my anger and frustrations, from an impetuous idealism, a subtle desire for prestige and power and domination? Or does it come from the love of God, from his word, from the Holy Spirit? I must challenge these impulses and feelings and projects and enthusiasm. Are they from my authentic spirit, the very core of me, from the Holy Spirit who moves in peace along the ways of love? A strong question.

Lorraine further encouraged me. "Instead of giving yourself to a round of activity, of surface prayer speaking shallow thoughts, rather tune in on your depths where God truly works, consult your authentic spirit. Be your authentic self, speak your authentic core out to God. You are a special and sacred word-of-God-made-flesh. He loves you as you are. He spoke your name and created you as a unique person. So be who you are as created by God. In prayer say your own word, sing your own song and be true to it."

# 9

# Summer of 1982

## A Humbling Experience

It's early May and time for my junior CLC group to make our closed retreat along Lake Michigan in our A-frame cabin. We plan a prayer retreat with significant sharing. One morning became a humbling experience but one I'm deeply grateful to God for. Each of us filled out a paper with three columns: major events of our life so far, major persons who entered our lives, and times when God moved in a special way into our conscious lives.

Here are some quotes from the CLC lads:

"What can I say to the man who has changed my life. You are responsible for everything good I have going in my life, for my faith life. God loves you, and so do I, and that is from my heart." —Jeff

"You are the main reason that I have a strong faith life and a strong prayer life. I think God reaches me through my friends, my CLC group, my family, but most of all God reaches me through you." —Steve

"Your faith in God is something which I admire. You really don't care about anything else, and so it should be. I want you to know that you have changed my life and shaped it towards God." —Brian

"I always wanted to tell you how I feel. You have really helped make the living God present to me. It truly frightens me

when I wonder what I would be like today if we had never met early that September morning in our chapel after the Eucharist. Without you I never would have grown and matured in Christ as I have. I had a strong faith before I met you, but it was somewhat superficial. Now I can say in all certainty and sincerity I have a living faith with deep, deep roots. You mirror the Lord to me, and his love and grace truly emanate from you."
—Tom

## To sing my own song. No, God's song.

It's late May, 1982, time for a much-needed retreat. For my retreat master I picked Fr. Gene Merz, head of the renewal effort in our province. For years fellow Jesuits had told me what a marvelous spiritual director and retreat guide he was, how strong and direct and sensitive a man he was. In talking with him in January, I was impressed by his spiritual depth, his sense of our Jesuit justice thrust based on that spiritual depth. I approached that retreat with a sense of deep need.

Right from our first conference we meshed on a deep level. He sensed intuitively where I was and met me there. I cued him in on how the last year had gone and where I found myself going in this retreat. It had been a very difficult spring for me. So much turmoil and frustration to process in April and May. For five years we theology teachers had tried many different ways of implementing the call to work on structural injustice as voiced by Arrupe's *Men for Others,* as enunciated in the Society's famous Fourth decree of 1975 on the promotion of faith and justice. Finally three of the four sophomore theology teachers put together a plan: team-teaching a full academic quarter on poverty here at home, on hunger and poverty and oppression in the Third World, on the nuclear war threat and the arms race. We brought in knowledgeable speakers, showed the best of the movies available, held a number of assemblies for the whole sophomore class on special social justice issues, instituted an experiential project for all sophomores to help at St. Benedict's inner-city meal program, and capped it with a retreat which featured a world hunger meal. The whole thing was integrated around the mission of the Christian as given in baptism and confirmation. This cost the three of us untold planning, scheduling, and hard work. It was creative. For a first effort it went remarkably well. The majority of our students accepted it and seemed quite appreciative of our efforts. Some lads felt it was one-sided, but they were a minority, and we tried to deal sensitively with them.

In April, however, at the end of the quarter on justice, at a meeting with our department head, the blow fell. He had picked up criticism from some students and from two faculty members. Without conducting a professional evaluation of our students and their reaction, he dropped this bomb. "You rammed it down their throats, too much for their developmental level." We protested, but he maintained his position.

I was stunned. Our final effort as the result of five years of trial and error, so much of ourselves invested in the program, and then to have this judgment slapped on us. This effectively blew the whole program apart. I felt sharp disappointment and anger and frustration and real disillusionment. For a day or two I seriously considered leaving this high school I loved and had worked so hard for through twenty-three years and going into parish work in Oregon. It seemed to me that it was impossible to do much on structural injustice in this school, in this province, with these people. But then over the next two months, with the help of a sensitive assistant principal, things were modified and clarified. A written evaluation from our students on the justice quarter proved to be overwhelmingly positive; many spoke of their gratitude for what we had done and urged us to continue; a small percentage voiced disagreement. The criticism was scaled down and resulted in a good critique of the program. The administration gave a strong endorsement of our efforts and our ability as teachers along with some reflections on improving justice education. This restored my desire to keep on teaching here and do what I could.

But it was a dark shadow over a hard year's work, a tough ending to what had been a creative program. We knew that never again would we attempt such an effort. The project was dead in the water. The teacher who had initiated the idea and pushed for it was disaffected and left teaching. The whole experience left me rather disillusioned about the prospects for any resolute justice education at Marquette High. Perhaps high school students, especially sophomores, are simply too young for this. Perhaps our student body is too conservative, given the climate in the country in '82 and the clientele we increasingly drew from; perhaps justice and peace issues must be muted so as not to alienate our constituency. Maybe in the years to come there will be some implementation of the justice emphasis we are called to as a Jesuit school, but I felt sure it would be done cautiously and slowly. The gap between our rhetoric and our reality is great. I can still do something, but now I must be very careful. I felt progressively blocked and stifled, unable to voice in a significant way with freedom the story and the insights and the awareness and the knowledge I had so laboriously acquired over the last years. And the gnawing feeling: maybe the whole Third World experience, the track I had taken for eight years and felt to be God's providence in my life was simply a mistake and a wrong track. It had put me out of step with my world and led to so much trouble in my life. Why not trash the whole thing?

I poured out this hurting mess. Then I told Gene about the other pole in my life, how since 1971 at John's tomb and then with my first directed retreat, I have had a strong set of religious experiences which called me and continue to call me to a total gift of self to God, to a deeper prayer life and a much different kind of prayer. I explained Lorraine's statement from last year's retreat, "John, you have an authentic call to the very person of God." Yet all this seems to come to naught in the course of a busy high school year. It's always rush, rush; I'm swamped with details clamoring to be cared for; each year I get progressively tensed and fatigued. Even though I get up early in the morning and try to pray to God for an hour daily, the prayer never seems to go anywhere. Yet this call within me to the person of God gets more insistent each year. My inability to make any kind of complete response is a source of deep frustration. I'm fifty-six years old and feel that I should set out on a far more serious quest of this Lord in my life.

These two poles, the pull toward the Lord and the junk that stumbles around in me, contradicting poles it seems, all this I explained to Gene. Then I stopped. I felt he had heard me; at last someone knows instinctively what I am saying and feeling. In measured words he said: "John, you're at a very important time in your life. A decisive time, a time that will have an effect on your life for many years." He went on: "Our God is the God of enormous fidelity; he loves you. He's chosen you out for his intimate friend. He moves into your life strongly with freedom whenever he wants, however he wants. He'll never let you go. He keeps on and will keep on doing so." And then an earthy remark, "God doesn't wait till we get our shit together. He's the God of long-lasting, faithful love. He brushes aside your inner poverty, the messes inside you, and comes to you again and again. He will come at you sideways and blindside you when you least expect it. You're a poor man who has been richly loved. So face the fact; open yourself to him; let him touch your heart; get in touch with your depths; be willing to move any way he wants; go his way. None of these things in your life happens by accident; it's all part of the marvelous providence of God; trust that providence."

But a caution: "Look, the weak point in your armor is your suspicion that this experience since 1971 is an illusion. Your temptation's to think that all this is not really significant, not really worthwhile; God can't be that interested in you because of the messes inside. This's the way the evil spirit'll work most successfully in your life to make you doubt what God's done, to see it as unreal. The enemy wants you to look at just yourself, your unworthiness, not at God's love and his desire for you. No, John, what's going on in you is an authentic movement, God-initiated. Take these graces seriously. God's love for you, what he's done for you; these are unshakable realities."

Needless to say I felt relieved, consoled, so buoyed up, as though my way was coming clear. I thanked him for listening so carefully, for his affirmation. His comment was merely, "Look, all the pieces were there, scattered around; all I had to do was put them together and put words on it."

That afternoon, I prayed on the scripture Gene gave me and was amazed to hear the words of Isaiah 54 open up and enter into my soul. They met me where I was.

> Though the mountains may depart,
> Though the hills be shaken,
> My love will never leave you.
> My love-pact with you will never be shaken.
> With everlasting love I have taken pity on you.

I thought of the Jewish people and their travail at the time of Isaiah. How they were called by Yahweh and then were conquered, broken, deported, their city and temple destroyed, their dream ruined. I thought of our call as Christians to build God's world in justice and peace, to feed the hungry and care for the poor, and build the unity of the planet. Then I thought what had happened the last few years with the Reagan Administration: world hunger and human rights on a back burner, arms callously poured into El Salvador and Honduras, an Archbishop murdered, nuns and priests slain for their option for the poor, Guatemala slaughtering the lovely highland Indian people, an arms race wildly escalating, the fate of the earth in doubt, the hungry and the poor here in the U.S. cut off from aid in the name of GNP: a world so grim, an age of lunacy that must apparently run its course, the reversal of all our hopes. I thought of the death of our own dream of justice education of the young at Marquette High. The mountains and the hills, symbols of permanence, are shaken. Yet in the midst of all this, in Israel's history and in every age, only one thing is constant, only one thing is to be relied on: God's love will endure, his covenant will never fail.

I began to be at peace, content to follow God's providence along the dark way he leads, confident of his everlasting love and care. My life is set on what is truly unshakable.

Before bed I went before the Lord in the dark chapel and prayed the text again. I felt the Lord strongly drawing me to himself once again. This I rested in, asking him to attract me more and draw me to himself. Close to the tabernacle I prayed a longer time, feeling very close to him. Then I walked out into the night and the sky and the moon and the stars. Words of Psalm 90 came to me. "From everlasting to everlasting, you are God." Our lives come and go, wax and wane but you are the great God. It seemed the Lord was talking directly to me:

"John, no matter what happens, though everything seems to go awry with you and your world, I do love you. I have claimed you for my own, early in your life. I've done it again and again, more and more insistently. My love for you will never stop. I chose you for my own, I'll never let you go. We are joined in a love pact that is eternal, till the stars burn out."

At last I accepted this fact. "I'm yours forever, God, all the way to the end of my life. I'm your priest. I'll seek you all the days of my life. Just keep on drawing me, give me a hunger for you that grows, the hunger and drawing that I feel tonight. We are yoked together like husband and wife, in a love-pact that will stand no matter what happens in the world outside. You love me even though I'm foolish and shallow and weak. That doesn't matter to you. You bend to me and want me. So I say yes for good. To you, the God of the sky and the moon and stars, the everlasting God. An everlasting marriage. You call me with an all-wise providence, none of this by chance. And so superior-ship and Guatemala and all that has happened—none of it by chance. You ask me to love you and to respond to your call one step at a time, leaving results in your hands."

It's Pentecost Sunday, that day when the Spirit came like a powerful wind shaking the house where the Apostles were, descending on them like flames of fire. I pray that the Holy Spirit may come to me, help me let go of the junk in the past, the frustration, the hurt, and open a new path that I may travel it in joy and say yes to him in the middle of my life. I walk out in the morning and the words of the Pentecost Office speak perfectly my desires.

> "My heart and my flesh cry out for the living God.
> O God, you are my God whom I seek;
> Your kindness is a greater gift than life.
> Drench our dried-up lives with your grace
> Free our restless hearts;
> Give us your peace."

That morning I puzzled over the path ahead. How should

I serve God in the years to come? Should I keep slogging along the same old route, doing the same things? Wouldn't I suffer growing irritation and boredom and frustration? Am I trapped in the wrong spot, the wrong work? Should I change ministry and find new work? Should I change the focus of the work I'm in? How can I follow the deep bents of my person and best express them?

In my conference with Gene, he suggests: "Look, the movement that's been going on in you is authentic; take these graces seriously; they're God's great gift to you, a rich story. Why not take what's closest to your heart, what God's done in you all these years and relate this to others? Why not write an autobiography, a journal-type thing, and simply tell the story of what God's done in you. Look at Teilhard, such riches inside and yet he was forbidden to teach and publish. But after his death, through his writings, he could reach a wide audience and touch so many people. Yes, John, why not do it?"

A new idea, and it germinated. As the afternoon went on, I felt increasingly that this was the key. Peace came to me more and more. At last someone listens and takes the whole story seriously and puts a name on it: "God's great gifts to you, treasure them!" This proposal seems so right. To write a journal-type book, to break out of the narrow confines where I am hedged in with so many restrictions and *caveats* to speak at last of what is closest to my heart and perhaps touch many other hearts, to take the graces I've been given and relate them to whoever is interested, to do something like Nouwen's *Genesee Diary*, a frank journal that deeply touched me.

Now the impasse is broken, the logjam of frustration is gone. The new path is suddenly clear. Yes, it all does lead somewhere. There is a steady Providence leading me, all things do work for good if a person loves God. Peace grows as I ponder this new path so suddenly opened. Then a growing sense of inner freedom mounts in me, a rising tide of joy and spontaneity before the Lord. And prayer is easy and flows like a river. Nature around me speaks of God. Scripture comes alive and nourishes me.

I read Mary's *Magnificat* and listen to the little handmaiden of the Lord sing her joy out to her Lord:

"My soul proclaims the greatness of the Lord.
My spirit exults in God my Savior.
He has looked with mercy on my lowliness.
His mercy reaches from age to age,
And Holy is his name."

I feel a quiet gentle joy in what the Lord has done. Yes, I feel strange in saying God has done great things for me; she after all is Mary, God's mother. But I know in my bones that this God has done special things for me. I've always known it. So why not say it as if I meant it. It's all God's doing, not mine. Yes, like Mary, I do want to sing my own song at last. That phrase becomes key for the years ahead: "To sing my own song at last."

But Gene modifies that: "No, John, not your song; God's song in you, the song he's been singing in you for years."

What a freeing thing. The whole story bottled up in me and no way to express it; I came to feel that my story was useless, and I almost believed it. Now, at last, an avenue is open. I can leave something of myself behind me.

This afternoon my heart comes awake and takes off and soars like an eagle. Peace and joy stream like glad tides into my soul. Prayer once again becomes easy, effortless; I can't get enough of it. I'm drawn to the Eucharist with a palpable hunger, to be with the Lord close to him. I'm nourished by each scripture I take up: Mary's Annunciation and her wide-open yes to the Spirit; the Holy Night when the young mother treasured all these things and pondered them in her heart. Lord, help me to treasure your gifts to me and to sing your song.

The words of Luke 6:35-38 became alive and spoke strongly to me: "Love your enemies, do good to those who hurt you. ... Be compassionate as your heavenly Father is compassionate, don't judge others and you won't be judged, don't condemn others and you won't be condemned, grant pardon and you will be pardoned, give and there will be gifts for you. ... The amount you measure out will be the amount you will be given back."

That night I rode my bike out into a cloudy, cool evening. As I came back near the lake, a great slash of crimson light cut along the western horizon. It grew to glory as the setting sun dipped below the cloud cover. I got to the Point as the sun's rays slanted and touched the whole world gold. My Walkman was playing the exuberant "Chariots of Fire," just the right music for this night. Waves borne in on a strong night wind crashed against the shore. The wild sunset lasted for only five precious minutes. I gloried in such moments of exultation. The crimson flood lingered for a long time and brought the retreatants out to the lakefront in silent wonder at the spectacle.

The words came back to me: "He who fashioned the heart of each." Yes, God fashioned my heart and my soul the way it is; I'm attracted to God as beauty; he gave me a heart that quickens and soars like shafts of light spearing through clouds, an ecstatic spirit in whom joy courses freely. Yet, I'm unable to voice the spirit well and share it with others. People tend to laugh and poke fun at it; but it can only be who I truly am, the way God made me.

By nature I am mystic, poet, sensitive to beauty. When that's not accepted, it gets me depressed.

The next day I biked against a strong north wind in the glory of a cold front and came to my "sacred spot," a farmer's lonely meadow, surrounded by forest, with a stream flowing through it; there in the meadow I lifted my face to the God of creation and reverenced him. I adored him, Father and Son and Holy Spirit. Than I lay before him face down in prayer as a beggar and a sinner asking for all my needs; then I lay on my back open to the sun, asking him for the greatest possible openness of spirit, giving myself to him as I am and being quiet in that self-surrender. I felt very at home in the middle of nature under the open sky. There were breathtaking moments when the wind, the breath of the creation, blew and rippled the long grass and the whole of nature seemed to vibrate with God present. And I was part of this universe, one with it.

After a while I opened Luke's Gospel to chapter twelve and asked the Holy Spirit to open Scripture to me and speak through that word. Suddenly there it was: his living word coming strong into my mind and heart and filling me. How striking it was to walk in the grass barefoot after shedding my clothes and to hear the Lord say: "Why worry about your clothing, what to put on or what to eat?" Overhead an eagle or big hawk soared, effortlessly playing off the wind. "Look at the birds of the air, God takes care of them." I walked through lovely yellow spring flowers sprinkling that meadow, splendid in their glory. "God takes care of all of them; how much more will he take care of you?"

Yes, God knows me, inside and out, he knows my needs, he has great care for me, a fifty-six-year providence which is going somewhere, which has led me to this precious moment where at last I have something to say, maybe the work of a lifetime beginning now; yes, follow his lead, be open to it. Seek God's kingdom, he'll take care of all the rest. Walk this new way, his way.

For an hour and a half I stayed there, feeling so much at home with my Lord, endlessly nourished by Luke's words. Then I rode back to the retreat house with a settled peace and quiet enveloping me. Twice I went into chapel and came close to Jesus and asked him to draw me to himself. I felt love flaming out and hunger and thirst for him growing. That whole evening was so calm and peaceful and healthy. I felt healthier than ever before and poised and sure in the Lord. And all this without effort, just being with God and experiencing little rivers of joy and desire suddenly starting in me.

At breakfast the next morning, they played Talbot's "For the Bride," a musical presentation of the Song of Songs. God the lover, his bride, their ecstatic union. Again I felt the fire of desire flaming out to him, for God alone, to center my whole life on him. Whenever I went to visit the Lord, I experienced the same inner surge to him. And so the retreat went.

Some final directions were solid and good: Gene's advice to be quiet before the Lord; a new way for me of being with the Lord, quiet wordless communion like a husband and wife before a fireplace. Silence first, being with the Lord, and words coming only out of that quietness. It's as though the Lord were saying to me, "If you're finished talking, now just be quiet and let me be God and let me speak to you."

A passage from Paul that Gene directed me to was most significant:

> Nothing can outweigh the supreme advantage of knowing
> Jesus Christ; for him I have accepted the loss of everything:
> I look upon everything as so much rubbish if only I can have
> Christ; all I want is to know Christ and the power of his
> resurrection and to share his suffering by reproducing his
> death-resurrection pattern. Let us go forward on the road
> that has brought us to where we are.

Gene's caution was to expect the cross of suffering. "It's the
sign of Jesus, welcome it; it's the way in which he purifies you,
his seal on your path." His final quote as I left the retreat was
Paul's words to Timothy: "Fan into flame the gifts that God has
given to you."

Deeply grateful for these precious days, filled with God's
grace, peaceful and joyful, I drove home to Milwaukee conscious of the new path I was to travel. I waited four months,
testing the graces and then drew up a formal proposal for my
superior and the school administration, explaining in four
typed pages the process that led to my proposal. I asked to have
my class schedule cut back to three classes daily, to be ex-
empted from hall prefecting assignments, to be finished therefore by noon each day. I made this request to have more time for
reflection and for prayer, so that I might seriously write this
journal.

I spoke also of my desire to reroute to more adult work and
so take up two Masses each Sunday at a new parish outside
Waukesha, to devote myself more to adult spiritual direction
and some adult directed retreats and CLC work. I was gratified
by the response: the provincial staff people, my own rector, and
the school administration warmly encouraged me and agreed
to the new schedule. It brought me to life and engaged my
creativity and tapped what was growing white-hot in me.

## Who Am I?

Two weeks after the retreat, I flew to Halifax, Nova Scotia,
for two weeks of PRH, a Jungian-Rogerian self-development
program in Canada. The heart of the experience was the basic

course "Who Am I?", an attempt to track down one's inner self
that God created us to be. For four days we followed ten
imaginative, indirect tracks into that reality. We then were to
take two hours, go apart and contemplate this inner self we had
unveiled.

I walked down the hill in the morning sunshine reading
over the eight traits that seemed most to make up who I am.
This exercise reinforced the insights and thrust of my retreat.
Once again joy and spontaneity and gratitude and peace and a
sense of solidity were mine. This is what I wrote that day:

"Who am I? My inner self:

1) I am a person whose very deep desire is for the living
God, who experiences a steady call to the depths initiated by
God.

2) I am a person who has an instinctive love for young
people. I am warm, encouraging and compassionate, loving
them for their fresh goodness and potentiality.

3) I am a person whose desire is to bring God and deep life
to the young, who thrills to this whenever it happens: in Eucharist, in Reconciliation, in prayer, in nature.

4) I am a person who has a pronounced mystic, poetic strain
that goes very deep: a sense of the ecstatic, the innocent, the
oneness of things, a glad joy in creation, extra sensitive to
beauty in nature, in music and poetry and literature, in young
people, in the rich river of joy running at the heart of life.

5) I am a person who has an instinctive love for the poor and
oppressed of the world, a drive to find out the structural causes
that oppress so as to build God's world in justice and peace, to
bring this awareness to young people.

6) I am a person whose temperament is enthusiastic, to be
an activist, impatient with deadheads and dawdlers.

7) I am a person who is trying to grow in personal warmth
and compassion and peace of heart and mellowness as I move
into the late fifties.

8) I am a person who is in process, changing both gradually
and dramatically to new things, to more depth with God, with
others, with the young, to more solitude, more prayer, deeply
eager to sing my own song at last—rather, God's song in me."

This inner self is the deeper self created by God in uniqueness. For me then, the job is to walk in my own shoes, to travel my own journey, to take responsibility for my own life, to be the person God made to be.

At the end of that institute, I slung a knapsack on my back and set out on a hitchhiking tour of New Brunswick province to track down the haunts of the clan on my mother's side. I spent days on lovely Prince Edward Island, bicycling its outer coast, swimming its rocky coves and beaches, sampling the flavor of its hearty people. For me hitchhiking is a spiritual experience, putting myself each day in the hands of a benevolent Providence and trusting what comes. And it came: friendly people on the road, great conversations, marvelous luck. I loved it.

# 10

## 1983, an Eventful Year

### Brush with Death

Another school year, this one much more satisfying. A year of letting go, a year of growing freedom, a year that had seen my proposal on a new path approved and a beginning made. It's now May 7, and I'm in Watertown, west of the city, for the wedding of my former CLC lad. The school year is almost done, but I find that I am terribly fatigued and I can't figure out why. We celebrate a beautiful wedding for Jerry and his bride at the local Episcopalian Church. I leave the party around 10 P.M. and head for home, very tired, blinking back sleep. On the freeway ten miles from Marquette High, I fall asleep on the wheel.

I woke up suddenly to a terrible bouncing. I'd gone off the freeway, my left wheel had mounted the divider. Dead ahead loomed a concrete pillar coming at me at 55 mph. Somehow I wrenched the wheel and got the car off the divider. It ground to a sudden halt on the left shoulder and I sat there shaken. No blood anywhere, nothing hurt; I searched for my glasses and found them beneath the seat and got out. A carload of college kids pulled in front of me. "Are you okay?" "I guess so." Then they said, "Father, there must be somebody up there taking special care of you. We thought for sure you would be killed. Do you know what you did? You went off the road and climbed the divider, got off it just as you got to the pillar, and then went right back up on it, and then down again." They couldn't believe how lucky I had been.

The car didn't look too bad—a flat tire, not much apparent damage, but the whole frame was severely sprung. At length the tow truck arrived. The beefy driver had this to say on the way home. "You know, Father, you're really lucky. Most of the time when people go up on the divider, the car rolls over and over, and the driver dies. The good Lord must be saving you for something important." I swallowed hard.

I left the car in the driveway, and feeling good, I went into our senior prom and greeted our lads and their dates and then slept like a log. The next morning I awoke glad to be alive, so grateful to God. Morning never looked better. By then the reality of that night had dawned on me. At fifty-seven I almost died on the freeway. Intimations of mortality. Imagine, on May 7, my life done; all my projects and appointments canceled; the story closed and me facing the Lord. How rich a gift this one day of life seemed to me that morning. How many years do I have left? Psalm 90 came back. "We last no longer than a waking dream. We are like weeds that sprout in the morning, that grow and burst into bloom, that dry up and perish in the evening." Our life is so short; it fades away like a whisper. Lord, fill us each morning with your constant love so that we may sing and be glad all the days of our life.

What shall I do with the years I have left? I want to center my life on God, to introduce the young to the person of this God and to initiate them into personal relationship with him, to foster growth and happiness in all whose lives I touch by the gift of my warmth and friendship. The words of John XXIII come back to me: "In the few years I have left, I want to be a holy pastor. My days must be one long prayer. Prayer is to be the very breath of my life." A sobering evening and a sobering period of reflections for days afterward.

## John, Age 82

On June 19, at a large Father's Day party with a family I knew well, I met a grand old man, John, age eighty-two. His face breathed warmth and joy and richness of spirit. I was drawn to him and we talked at length. John told me: "In the morning when I get up, I thank God with all my heart for another day, for all the gifts of my life. If I have some pain, I thank God it's not a great pain. At night I thank God on my knees for his goodness to me. I don't ask God for anything anymore. I just thank him for everything. Years ago I decided on this and this is the way I live." He said this with such warmth and evident sincerity and joy that I was deeply moved. John, the diabetic, John whose beloved wife had died twenty-two years ago: such a mellow presence, his life a singing gratefulness to God. Every encounter with John since has been a grace-filled time for me.

## Thomas Merton, Contemplative

And then the surprise of the summer. So many summers I had spent in Montana amid the mountain country I loved so much. This summer was different by necessity. As a result of a bicycle accident, my right knee had been injured painfully the preceding October. The pain flared up three different periods, resulting in six weeks in a cast. Once again a purifying thing, throwing me more deeply on the Lord alone. Surgery was scheduled for June and then called off. Strangely, the leg got stronger after the day I walked into Lake Michigan and let the cold water cure me. That and walking the sandy shore were restorative. My doctor shook his head. However, this disability curtailed my mountain climbing activities and kept me close to home for the summer.

As luck would have it, I signed up for a week at Retreats International at the University of Notre Dame, a popular summer program in spirituality. My course was the "Spirituality of Thomas Merton" by Jim Finley. Jim had been a Trappist for six years and had the good fortune of having Thomas Merton as his spiritual director. He then left the Trappists, married, was the proud father of two children, and is now doing doctoral studies in psychology and spirituality at UCLA. His book, *Merton's Palace for Nowhere*, on contemplation according to Merton, I had read and enjoyed. Jim, I found, was an excellent lecturer: clear, humanly paced, gently humorous, with a knack for anecdotes that truly illuminated. I found that I took twenty-eight pages of notes from five days of his class; the material he gave was something I had wanted for years. It gave me a conceptual underpinning for what I was experiencing inside; it put names on things I was feeling deeply; and it provided me with a great thrust forward on the path I had embarked on. A grace coming to me out of the blue, the high point of the year.

From so many things that spoke directly to me, I'll single out four themes which have had a continuing influence on my life.

### The True Self

One of the great fruitful themes Finley presented was an element of Merton's basic anthropology, his doctrine of the true self. I believe it is an insight that comes from his own mystical experience and articulates that. As such, it resonated immediately with me as a precious insight, one that squared eminently with my own experience of God and made sense. It goes something like this:

The true self is what God first creates in us. He creates a person, a capacity for himself, the so-called spiritual "me." God in himself is all fullness, a fullness that wants most deeply to share his Trinitarian riches of being and intimacy and love and joy. And so out of his boundless love he creates me, a created capacity for himself so that he can share himself and all he is with me. My true self, then, is basically my bare existence as person, which is a created capacity for the infinite God, like an empty pitcher. A pitcher has one function, to be filled with orange juice or beer or Bloody Marys. It is stamped "capacity: five cups." So I am stamped "capacity God." This then is the true self that the Father forever loves. This is the true self hidden in Christ which only the Father knows. This is the self whose one central activity is to receive and respond to divine love. In my depths I am a relation of love to the God whose name is love, the Beloved.

God first creates capacity for himself in me. So our destiny, then, is to become filled with God. God discovers this emptiness, this nothingness; it is his ecstasy, his rapture, his total delight to pour his whole being into that emptiness and fill it. Suppose you have a farm in the country, an immense pasture, and a great black stallion. After work you drive home in your sports car and let that great stallion loose. All day long he has been chafing, restless to get out. He runs and runs in that pasture with enormous delight, filling it with his presence. We are that pasture, God is the great stallion whose delight is to run and run in us and fill us with his presence.

Who awakens this awareness of our true self? It is the Spirit. So in my personal history there comes the blessed moment when the Spirit seeks me out, touches me in my heart, gives me a moment where I experience this God and know that I am in his presence. My emptiness is addressed, my depths are uncovered, and desire and attraction are awakened for God. This is almost always a surprise for a human being, something unplanned, not on the radar. It is God finding me in my ordinary life. At that moment, my spiritual life, my life with God begins, a dynamic journey in quest of this God. From then on, the challenge of this journey is to live in fidelity to this awakening, to live on the level of the depths uncovered. This is exactly what Lorraine meant when she said "an authentic call to the very person of God." A call to our true self in God, to our depths.

This first touch, unpredictable, has been renewed again and again during the story of my life, in moments of awareness, times both gentle and intense, subtle and obvious, through both absence and presence experiences, ache and ecstasy, emptiness and fullness. Each is a renewed invitation to the very person of God, an awakening to a reality that is always there, slumbering in our depths. It's like God saying to us: "Gotcha!"

This true self is perhaps best described by Merton himself in a passage that has come to have very deep meaning for me:

> Again that expression, *le point vierge*, (I cannot translate it) comes in here. At the center of our being is a point of nothingness which is untouched by sin and by illusion, a point of pure truth, a point of spark which belongs entirely to God, which is never at our disposal, from which God disposes of our lives, which is inaccessible to the fantasies of

our own mind or the brutalities of our own will. This little point of nothingness and of absolute poverty is the pure glory of God in us. It is, so to speak, his name written in us, as our poverty, as our indigence, as our dependence, as our sonship. It is like a pure diamond blazing with the invisible light of heaven. It is in everybody, and if we could see it we would see these billions of points of light coming together in the face and blaze of a sun that would make all the darkness and cruelty of life vanish completely. ... I have no program for this seeding. It is only given. But the gate of heaven is everywhere ... if only every body could realize this! But it cannot be explained. There is no way of telling people that they are all walking around shining like the sun.

Each one of us is shadowed, of course, by an illusory person, the false self. That false self is the illusion of my separate self as an absolute, as a center of the universe, the hub of the bicycle wheel. I rationalize that this egocentric self, this self of mine that I project to others, is the fundamental reality of life to which everything else in the universe is ordered. So I can spend a whole life up on the surface, winding experiences around myself, covering myself with pleasure and possessions and bodily beauty and strength to make myself visible and important to myself and my world. I clothe this superficial self and try to construct its nothingness into something real. And I can use a whole lifetime doing this, meanwhile ignoring my depths. But under all these things with which I am clothed, I am hollow. My structure of pleasure and ambitions has no foundation. I am a mistake. This is the radical mistake of life, to ignore one's true self, the self created by God, the growing capacity for him who is our destiny.

### The Cosmic Dance

The cosmic dance of the universe is perhaps best articulated in the last three paragraphs of *New Seeds of Contemplation*, Merton's most popular and best-loved book. The basic image is a favorite of the mystics, the image of God as a bridegroom dancing with his bride, that is, all of his creation, at a wedding feast. How often we've seen at a wedding reception the bridegroom with an enormous smile and tender love sweep his bride into his arms and out onto the dance floor; then the other couples follow. So also our cosmic God of creation. He is so deeply in love with his whole creation, especially us his rational creation, that he is engaged in a joyous dance daily with us, the work of his hands. This dance is going on all the time around us and in us, in every breath we draw and in every heartbeat. To live fully then is to tap into this reality that lies below the surface of things and to touch this rich river of joy and love that is being poured out into our world. Here is Merton at his best:

> What is serious to men is often very trivial in the sight of God. What in God might appear to us as "play" is perhaps what he himself takes most seriously. At any rate the Lord plays and diverts himself in the garden of his creation, and if we could let go of our own obsession with what we think is the meaning of it all, we might be able to hear his call and follow him in his mysterious cosmic dance. We do not have to go very far to catch echoes of that game and of that dancing. When we are alone on a starlit night; when by chance we see the migrating birds in autumn descending on a grove of junipers to rest and eat; when we see children in a moment when they are really children; when we know love in our hearts; or when, like the Japanese poet Basho, we hear an old frog land in a quiet pond with a solitary splash, at such times the awakening, the turning-inside-out of all values, the newness, the emptiness and the purity of vision that make themselves evident, provide a glimpse of the cosmic dance.

> For the world and time are the dance of the Lord in emptiness. The silence of the spheres is the music of a wedding feast. The more we persist in misunderstanding the phenomena of life, the more we analyze them out into strange finalities and complex purposes of our own, the more we involve ourselves in sadness, absurdity and despair. But it does not matter much, because no despair of ours can alter the reality of things, or stain the joy of the cosmic dance which is always there. Indeed, we are in the midst of it, and it is in the midst of us, for it beats in our very blood, whether we want it to or not.

Yet the fact remains that we are invited to forget ourselves on purpose, to cast our awful solemnity to the winds and join in the general dance.

Our problem, of course, is to free ourselves of compulsive rush, pouring ourselves out on surface things, on our ambitious projects. We can spend a lifetime on these. Or we can live in the past riddled by guilt at our mistakes, angry and bitter over what people have done to us, ceaselessly trying to puzzle out why things happened, spiraling down in self-pity and depression, despairing about people and the world around us. Or we can live in the future, crippled by anxiety over what may come: nuclear war, crime erupting in my neighborhood, economic downturn and loss of job, cancer and heart attack and all else. In short we can center on our selves, on absurdity and despair, and miss the one moment each of us has right here and now, the moment in which God is present and active and revealing himself: the moment of the cosmic dance.

Merton casts his spirituality in one stunning sentence: "The only true joy on earth is to escape from the prison of our false self and to enter into union with the life who dwells and sings within the essence of every creature and in the core of our own souls."

The day had been a hot 103 degrees. As the sun edged down and the heat subsided, I put on a T-shirt, hiking shorts and tennies, boarded my bike, and headed across the Notre Dame campus, past avenues of trees at St. Mary's, down a long dirt nature trail along the river, and out into the fields north of the campus. There I put down my bike, walked around reading McDonnel's *Merton Reader.* After a while I looked over at the sunset, and it was glorious that evening. Pastel cumulus clouds had settled in the west; through them great shafts of golden sunshine were breaking. I marveled to the spectacle and continued to read. Then I became aware of a long low line of purple clouds laced by lightning coming in from the Lake Michigan shore to the north. Suddenly a vehement gust of wind struck, whirling my cap off and sending it spinning into the fields. The branches of a big elm tree close to me tossed back and forth. Suddenly, I who love storms, was afraid of the thunder and the lightning in this open field and of being drenched by the storm, and unwilling to end my days at fifty-seven.

But then it dawned on me: this is the very cosmic dance Merton described. The wind tearing at my clothes, the dark clouds sailing overhead, the lightning and thunder all around me, the sunset now crimsoning out to the west: yes, this is the cosmic dance, the very ecstasy of creation, the rich river of joy at the heart of creation, the Lord's unique show for me. So for an hour I stayed there, entranced by it, reveling in the Lord present so dramatically, myself so obviously in his hands in the very center of the tempest. Not one drop of water fell; gradually the force of the storm subsided. In the darkness I biked across campus, dodging downed tree branches. A great elm lay across the driveway of our dormitory. There in Flannery Hall, I joined Vatican III, the evening wine, beer and popcorn party, and told Jim Finley I had just experienced the cosmic dance!

*Awareness: the Seeds Image*

This theme is found in *The Seeds of Contemplation*. Merton says that every moment and every event in my life plants something in my soul. Just as the wind blowing in the springtime carries with it thousands of winged seeds, so each moment carries with it germs of spiritual vitality that come to rest imperceptibly in my mind and soul. Most of these numberless seeds perish because we are not really aware, not prepared to notice much less receive them. Every expression of God's will is in some sense a seed of new life. For the inscrutable love of God seeks in every situation to awaken us. But we must learn to leave ourselves, to find ourselves, by yielding to the love of him who approaches us. If we were looking for God, every event and every moment could be a contact with him who is present and acting in our lives and in the world outside. Merton expresses this need for awareness in his typical eloquent prose.

> For it is God's love that warms me in the sun and God's love that sends the cold rain. It is God's love that feeds me in the bread I eat and God that feeds me also by hunger and fasting. It is the love of God that sends the winter days when I am cold and sick, and the hot summer when I labor and my clothes are full of sweat: but it is God who breathes on me

with light winds off the river and in the breezes out of the wood. His love spreads the shade of the sycamore over my head and sends the water boy along the edge of the wheat field with a bucket from the spring, while the laborers are resting and the mules stand under the tree.

It is God's love that speaks to me in the birds and streams; but also behind the clamor of the city God speaks to me in his judgments and all these things are seeds sent to me from his will. If these seeds would take root in my liberty and if his will would grow from my freedom, I would become the love that he is and my harvest would be his glory and my own joy. And I'd grow together with thousands and millions of other freedoms into the gold of one huge field praising God, loaded with increase, loaded with wheat. If in all things I consider only the heat and cold, the food or the hunger, the sickness or labor, the beauty or pleasure, the success and failure or the material good or evil my works have won for my own will, I will find only emptiness and not happiness. I shall not be fed, I shall not be full. For my food is the will of him who made me and who made all things in order to give himself to me through them.

The universe is truly a sacramental universe; that is, a universe that is a sign, a symbol, revealing the infinite God who made it. It is so for those who know how to see. Another way of putting it: all creation is word of God. The Lord in eternity thought it, and it came to be. Let there be light, and light penetrated creation. Let there be water, and water came to be. Let there be earth, granite, the bedrock of it, and there was earth. Let there be John Eagan, and John Eagan came to be. Let there be Peter, Tom, Mike, and there was Peter, Tom, Mike.

Each of us is a reality which enfleshes God's eternal, creative world. If I truly know how to see, I am in touch with God in all of his creation. Then the whole of creation speaks to me of this creating God. Each birch tree, each lad I teach, each eagle I watch, each lake I swim in—all concretize, enflesh God's word. The whole world is voicing God, is immersed in God.

That means, too, that a tree gives glory to God by being a tree. Being what it is, it consents to his creative love; the more a tree is itself in all its individuality, the more it is like God and expresses God. This particular tree will give glory to God by spreading its roots into the earth and raising its branches into the air and the light in a way that no other tree before it or after it ever did or will do. It gives glory to God by being precisely what he wants it to be here and now.

But what about human beings? What about me? You? It is true to say that for me my sanctity consists in being myself and for you your sanctity consists in being yourself. Your sanctity will never be mine, and mine will never be yours.

The problem of sanctity, then, is the problem of discovering my true self. And that once again brings us back to Merton's doctrine of the true self.

### God is No-thing

A final great moment of that Finley course remains. On the fourth morning, Jim was taking the standard apophatic approach to God. God simply is no thing. He is not a limited essence or thing that I can get a clear concept of with my mind. He simply explodes all limited categories, all the limited concepts of my mind. So he is the great *"Who Is'* "incomprehensible to the human mind, the infinite One. He is the only One whose essence is to be. He is simply the One who is all in all, the source, the ground of all being, the fulfillment of all that exists, the no thing that sustains all beings in existence and life.

This means that nothing that I see or touch or experience is God. God simply exceeds every living creature infinitely. And so I can move through the whole of creation as Augustine did and question each lovely creature: "Are you God?" and each creature, even religious experiences, will answer and say, "No, I am not God; he infinitely exceeds me." Not God—not God— not God. God alone is God. He is no thing. He is the only One who simply is; he is all in all.

I was struck by this. As I went to noon Mass with 400 other classmates, this thought was playing in my head like a tape. Not God, not God, not God, you God, you alone. As I came up to Communion and the celebrant gave me the Body of the Lord and I ate, suddenly it hit me: yes, finally, you God, you. It took my breath away. God himself, the great All, was with me. Astounded, overwhelmed by the sudden realization I came back and sat down silent with the wonder of it all. God who infinitely surpasses all that is, the God who is all in all, is with me now. I possess the All. Dazed, filled with wonder, conscious of God with me, adoring, grateful, my soul wheeled out for him in desire.

## The Advent of Diabetes

On September 10, my internist shocked me. "John, you are an adult onset diabetic." For six months or so I had been troubled with extensive fatigue, with a thirst I couldn't satisfy, and with sudden pressure to urinate. During the summer my doctor kept a wary eye on my blood sugar as it swung from 300 to 157 to 190. So on September 14, I sat down with a determined dietician at St. Joe's. Her prescription was stark: a whole change of lifestyle. Gone was booze, all booze; no pie, no cake, no more french fried food, no more chocolate-chip cookies, no rich gravies and hot fudge sundaes, no jams and second helpings. Instead an 1800-calorie diet featuring two fruit portions and lots of low-fat rabbit food, all in a strict balance, and daily exercise at least an hour and a half on my bike. The target was to go from a more than ample 192 to 160 pounds. I asked her what the alternative was. I didn't like what I heard: stroke, heart attack, hardening of the arteries, problems kidneys, blindness, eventual amputations: big trouble ten years down the road.

I thought back; for some years I have been having trouble with morning weakness and sweating, with some dizziness. The last two years the fatigue was especially notable and it puzzled me. What's wrong with me? Falling asleep at the wheel that May weekend was a dead giveaway. This diagnosis at first hit me like a slug in the gut: another limitation added to teeth and knee and hearing. The radical diminishments of age. Would I be able to change a whole lifestyle? Yet the more I reflected on it, the more it appeared to be a hidden blessing. For years I had talked about dropping brandy and rum at social occasions. Though I enjoyed it as social lubricant, the aftereffect was no good. It blunted my fine edge. Losing weight would be very good for me. I was easily twenty-five pounds overweight and this had to be a strain on the heart. Climbing stairs over in school was beginning to cause heavy breathing. For years I had been overeating: too many second helpings, too many sweets.

So I determined to take this new reality, to unwrap it carefully, and to find the good that the Lord had in store for me. I thought of Max Pearce's saying: "Everything is designed to bring us home, if only we would work with it." I recalled Teilhard de Chardin's famous statement in his sixties when first a heart attack rudely cut off his field work as a paleontologist and then a directive from the Holy Office in Rome forbade him to publish in philosophy or theology: "All this is forcing me back upon the one thing that is necessary. Everything that happens is worship." So I decided to view it positively, to see it as one more way the Lord was purifying my life, cutting my ties, detaching me radically, freeing me into perhaps a new thing, a resurrection.

In the weeks to come the weight went fast: the first ten pounds was water weight; the second ten also went fast as my system retooled. I did experience hunger pangs in midafternoon. But then one giddy day in late October I bicycled twenty-three miles in the crisp cool air of a lovely fall day and returned to weigh in at 158. The first time below 160 since age nineteen! My waist had shrunk from 38 to 33. My physical and psychic energy level also surged. I felt ten years younger and supremely alive!

## Biking as a Paradigm of Life

It's a glorious fall day: the air is crisp and cool, the blue sky above is rich and deep as I head out for my bike ride along the Parkway after school. I'm fatigued from the outlay of nervous energy teaching classes of juniors and seniors. I find myself thinking of the difficulties of the day: the balky teenager, the hassle with discipline, the wear and tear of daily routine. Old frustrations come up, and I chew on them again; recent frustrations rise, and I process them as I ride along. Consciously I shed the negative thoughts that tie my soul down: the sadness, the absurdities, the despair, the awful solemnity that can monopolize me if I'm not careful. I begin to notice the beauty about me and contemplate and center on what is now: the glory of a special fall day, of clouds and blue sky and the flaming end of another year. Joy begins to well up. On and on I bike along the river savoring it all, rejoicing in the Father, Son and Spirit dwelling within, the source of all the life around me, they who have over the years claimed my heart. Another memorable afternoon in the movement of the cosmic dance!

Strange how these typical bike rides become more and more this year a paradigm of my life and what's going on in the depths of me. I have come gradually to characterize my soul this year as a battleground in which I'm being pulled constantly by two forces. There's the dark side that occupies my thoughts and feelings: the impatience and anger of daily life that clamor for attention, the frictions of daily living in a large community, the longstanding frustrations I chew over and over without resolution. But now I catch myself and bring it all to a skidding halt. Stop! I've had enough; I pull clear of it.

Then there's the other side: strong sudden experiences where stabs of joy break in, tugs, pulls at my heart where feelings of desire for the immense God are deeply present within me, a tapping into the rich river of joy that runs right under the surface of ordinary life, like an undertow pulling me out beyond the shores of the gloomy ordinary into the depths where the Lord is. This year especially I'm experiencing all sorts of these tugs towards God, sudden awareness-times that come upon me in the course of each day. These I see as a subtle movement to God, a purification where things that used to bring satisfaction are slowly turning to dust, and as an invitation to God and God alone as the source of my life.

# 11

## "This Bi-polar Thing"

### The Dark, Negative Pole

The negative thoughts that flood in are like rotten funguses that fasten on my psychological life and grow into more rottenness if I let them, that drain away my strength and my happiness, that preoccupy me and can grow like a cancer and sour my existence. Most of all, they waste my time and leave me negative and cynical, a state I hardly enjoy.

What am I talking about? A few examples from 1983. Our provincial, a good man, comes for his yearly visitation; he is very kind to me personally. In a final talk to the community he's asked about injustice and peace concerns and refers to them as "that junk." Knowing looks dart around the room; in me and in others, there's an instant insight. This man for five years has done next to nothing on these concerns of many of us. The great issues of our day have come and gone, a resounding silence. And now it's completely obvious: nothing can be expected from the leadership of the province. Instead, just business as usual, running the institution, keeping the ship afloat, plumbers and electricians, not strong, innovative leadership.

So it's finally clear: we can hope for nothing from on top, save calls for interior renewal and more prayer. His talk had a baneful effect on my life and led to many depressing moments as I chewed it over. So it has come to this. For days it festered in my memory until I finally came to terms with myself. Yes, I'll stop reading the Jesuit rhetoric from our General Congregation on justice; we're choking on too much rhetoric. I shall not say much; I won't expect much from on top anymore. I'll seek God and go my own way, trying to do what I can. But this single event has and does cause me inner frustration and puzzlement and unhappiness. A ghost hard for me in my idealism to lay to rest.

More examples. That October, I received an emotional letter from a junior who believed I treated him unfairly and had hurt him. To no avail I tried to explain, but he could not see it and followed with another emotional letter. And this disturbing thing festered. Teaching high school juniors a theology course on Christology is a risky business, I find. I do want to give them the person of Jesus, a personal knowing and experiencing and loving and following, and I want to do it in depth. It goes well for the most part; but there is always the one character who siezes on one thing you do and turns off, who looks you in the eye and you can tell he dislikes you and your whole approach and may even venture to say it, the 8th-period character who comes three minutes late, who has the sneaky side comment, who tries clandestine conversation as you give a crucial presentation. Confronted in a disciplinary way, he goes balky and angry, and my impatience flares. Each year it seems there are two or three of these. They provide the atrocities that sour the teaching experience. I have high goals as a teacher; I insist on results and work and solid intellectual content; and I'm impatient and in a rush to achieve these goals. When I'm blocked or angry, frustrated feelings surge up and have their day.

Then there's inevitable friction of living with forty other men in the same religious community. A variety of individual personalities with an age spread from twenty-four to eighty-six. I live with a man who never greets me with a hello, who never stops to talk and be friendly, who manages a word or two at most when I speak to him. This gets to me. The older Jesuit who never really answers a serious question you put to him but who keeps on unloading the same timeless, unexamined cliches. The curt one who responds to friendly overtones with a remark that cuts you off somewhere between the ankles and the knees. The negative gang of four who gather over beer to lament how things are going downhill in the school and in the community, and this at length. Such negatism sours my day. The interminable conversations on Packers and Brewers and Warriors and NCAA and on and on; the computer chatter; the endless talk on the school and the piddly jockeyings for position. Why don't we who entered to love God and seek him and serve him in his people share our lives with God? Why this cultivated anonymity? Why keep each other at an arm's length? Why relate impersonally and so create an effective desert?

And always the sheer rush and push of high school life: the daily order: forty-five-minute periods, bells, deadlines and deadly meetings, prefecting, paper correcting; the incredible outlay of emotional and nervous energy in teaching teens that takes its toll in fatigue by November and March, the dismal months. One has to be careful to avoid a robot existence, going through it and doing things to get them done, a dehumanizing way to live.

The mid-life thing. I watched these years of my late fifties when things in which I took great delight and into which I poured much enthusiasm, seemed to go dead. Retreats and CLC work and camping trips I can no longer do because of diminishing energy. Other things like sports and games and routine counseling and committee work no longer interest me. There's an increasing dissatisfaction with all else other than God. At times there's a glimmer that a process of progressive purification is going on in me, that so much of self and what I invested myself in is turning to ashes before my very eyes.

## The Positive Pole

That's the dark side. At the same time there is the joyous, deep, positive pull to the living God which I experience consciously this year. I will try to explain what I mean.

I get up each morning around 5:30 and spend an hour or an hour and fifteen minutes in prayer. Around 6:00, I settle in before the Lord in the Blessed Sacrament and offer him my day and speak to him of needs, often just sitting there with the words, "You, Lord, you," or "God alone," as my mantra. Many times not much happens; I get distracted, tired, sleepy, and then go up to my room to read from a book that speaks to me of God or from scripture, or I write significant things in my journal. Not much that is truly significant happens during morning prayer; but at odd times during the day when I least expect it, suddenly I'm blindsided. Things speak to me of God: nature comes alive and throbs with his presence, people say and do things that move me deeply, sudden stabs and pulses of joy well up and flow on endlessly with freedom, and I feel the joy of creation and of the cosmic dance about me. I'm alive again in God. These counter-point the dark thoughts and pull me more deeply to the Lord who loves me. Such moments have more and more been privileged times when God has moved into my life closely. For example:

I walk out in the morning sun and pray the Divine Office. The second cup of coffee has done its magic, and I read the Psalms; time after time one line sails off the page and pulls me to the Lord. "If you but knew the gift of God, you would ask, and he would give you the living water ... springs of living water welling up in you to life everlasting." Or, "I will take away your heart of stone and give you a heart of flesh to love me with." Or, "They will be my people; I will be their God." Or, "I have counted all as rubbish so that Christ may be my wealth and that I may know the power of his resurrection. I want to know one thing: Christ," And always, "Like a deer thirsting for running streams, so my heart thirsts for you, the living God."

These experiences are like stumbling on hidden streams that suddenly flow clean and clear, the subtle deep movement within to God that my own infidelity and inner poverty and junk can't block. This tells me again and again the deepest current of my life is elsewhere and I must go my way.

My reading increasingly is a cue to the subtle movement within. "Lord, awaken me, you whose love burns beyond the stars; light the flame of my lantern that I may always burn with love." Merton's words always resonate: "May my bones burn and ravens eat my flesh if I forget you [contemplation]; may language perish from my tongue if I do not remember thee, O Zion, city of vision"; or, "God alone, faceless, unknown, unfelt, yet undeniably God." Or Paschal, "There is in every person an infinite abyss that can only be filled by the infinite God himself." Or St. Augustine, "Lord, give me yourself." And then the words of a personal hero, Pedro Arrupe, our Jesuit General. Stricken by a terrible stroke, he stood before 220 Jesuits at our congregation in Rome, unable to speak, leaning on a brother infirmarian while his speech of resignation was read. "More than ever I find myself in the hands of God. This is what I have wanted all my life from my youth. But now there is a difference; the initiative is entirely with God. It is indeed a profound spiritual experience to know and feel myself so totally in his hands."

On Sunday mornings I drive a half-hour west to the parish where I've begun to serve. The parishioners are marvelous, open people with a progressive pastor who believes the Church is all of us and invites his people to co-ministry and sharing. I work hard to prepare a homily on Jesus as source of life. Typically, I begin on Monday mulling over Scripture; by Saturday I've worked seven hours or so, being careful to distill the thoughts out of my own lived experience. My goal is to call up supremely alive moments in their lives and in mine, moments of contemplative wonder all of us have, since I believe with Rahner that we are all mystics at heart. I try to express God as the horizon of every life, to share the rich river of joy to lead us into a living relationship with himself. This word comes straight from my heart, and the people respond. My voice rises with conviction for at last I'm saying what I deeply want to say.

Then the Eucharistic prayer takes off, a shared refrain, and it becomes, as Eucharist for others so often does, an experience of the Lord. The people come up, hundreds of them: grandmas and grandpas with canes, little children, teenagers, young couples in love, mothers and fathers holding their children, careworn faces and happy faces—and suddenly in the midst of it all a wave of awe and gladness comes over me. I'm so very glad to be here doing this, this day. "The Body of Christ," "the Body of Christ," hundreds of times. I realize all over again: "My God, I'm giving Jesus Christ to each person." For a few moments I choke and can't say the simplest of words: "The Body of Christ." Soon the line of people is ended and the blessing given. I tell the people, "I want you to know I'm happy having

Eucharist with you." They begin to clap in appreciation, and the applause goes on. I can't believe it. I drive home riding on a cloud.

The following is from my Journal for Sunday, December 9, where I try to express the feelings from these parish Eucharists.

> At the Our Father, holding hands all around the Church looking at one another and singing the Our Father, suddenly the beauty of it all struck me, and I couldn't speak the words of the Our Father and almost lost it with a rush of emotion. A wild gladness to be here—the joy of the moment! This is what I am all about. No place on earth I'd rather be. Nothing else I'd rather be doing: to be saying Mass for people. And then at Communion time, as I broke and folded over the host and then held it up: insight. What on earth am I doing? This is Jesus. God's own Son, the One who stands before each human being and invites himself in —the great God of stars and skies in my hands, and I'm bringing him to people, jarred out of time and place into an awareness of Who, the great Who!
>
> Sense of wonder ...look at what I'm doing: Tom and Corinne all day long selling bonds and stocks and pushing sales never able to talk about what they want to, where their lives truly are—yet I—I can give my message to 800 people. I can spend my whole life speaking of the Lord and his way. An enormous opportunity! I felt this as I gave Communion to hundreds: I make this all possible; without me no Mass. Without me, no homily, offertory, Christ's special coming. Bringing him to 800 people and then I go home. What a vocation: to bring Christ to others, to make all this possible! We live right up on the edge of mystery. At times the veil lifts a bit, and we are overwhelmed.

There are other positive things like the stunning evening in October in Horicon Marsh. My favorite couple, Tom and Corinne, whom I married in 1976, pick me up in the afternoon, and we drive an hour north on a crisp fall day into the great marsh where some 300,000 Canadian geese fly in and pause on their way south. We hike into the fields close to the water and watch great waves of these majestic birds, 200 at a time, winging their way in. As sunset approaches, the wild primrose sky is filled with thousands of birds. The sound of the geese honking fills our ears, a sound I loved as a boy, standing with eyes skyward at the fall journeyers. Sunset deepens and the last bands of geese fly in to rest.

We dine at the Wild Goose Inn overlooking the marsh and talk of Merton and contemplation and Zen, and Cabernet Sauvignon has never tasted better. Then we drive in the dark on a lonely road into the middle of the marsh and step out of the car. It's a cloudless night, a million stars sparkle overhead, and the Milky Way runs riot down the middle of the sky. All around us from every side rises the chorus of thousands of wild geese calling out in the night. It's awesome and breathtaking; we listen in wonder: the Lord of primeval nature is so close. We wish the moment could never end. With a sigh we get into the car and drive home. But the moment lingers.

It's January and new snow blankets Milwaukee. I head out to a hilly seven-mile ski trail in the Kettle Moraine area. It's a clear, clean day with bright sunlight; the sky is rich blue and the sun sparkles on the new-fallen snow—glorious. With my Walkman playing Bach's violin concertos, I hit the trail vigorously. The beauty of sight and sound and the thrill of new snow and gliding through the forest catches me, and joy surges in my bones, the joy that runs like an electric current through creation. The cosmic dance again beats in my blood, and it goes on and on. I stop and listen to the silent woods and watch sun glint off light snow, and I'm glad to be in God's world and feel again movement to the center. The Lord of love at play, exulting in his creation.

In the afternoon I take pen and paper and continue writing the record of God's story in me, his gracious gifts in my life. I find this writing hard work: trying to order sections from my journal into a unified flow, to catch the exact word that crystalizes the experience. Yet I find the sheer attempt to voice the goodness of the Lord joyful and creative. Whenever I do this writing, I touch something of God, something that nourishes me and is lifegiving.

A final example. It's Ash Wednesday at Marquette High, and there's Eucharistic liturgy in the school gym, followed by the giving of ashes. Strange how this simple ritual brings our lads out of the floorboards as 900 show up. During Mass, I give the Body of the Lord to our boys: the Body of Christ to young Joe whom I teach, the Body of Christ to Tom whom I counsel, and so on. I could do this forever, bring Christ to his young. At the end of the Mass, I stand and sign the Lord's cross in ashes on the foreheads of hundreds. "Remember, Dave, you are dust and to dust you will return." Young faces, young eyes so clear, so fresh, so searching. They throng six deep as I trace the sign of the Cross on each forehead: young David, young John, young Michael, you with your quick intelligence, you with your whole life journey ahead of you, you with all your plans, you with the new girl friend, you pointed to the future like a swift arrow. Each of you came from the dust of the earth, and you move forward to return to that dust once more. How strongly it hits me: each of the hopeful young who engulf me this morning will wax and wane and then die. To dust—all. The poignancy and fragility of life hits me deeply as I look into the eyes of the tender young. The words "Remember..." choke on my lips. So many times as lads I know and like come up to me, I'm unable to complete the sen-tence in anything other than a whisper. Tears fill my eyes; I recover my voice somehow. On and on this experience goes until the bell rings, and we move to first period.

Life, the journey, the exile traveling to his true home. We come out from the creative hand of God and move into a short, fast journey on the face of the planet, traveling through time on the way to God. How fast the years go. Like the arrow's passage through the air, like the play on the stage, like spring flowers that push up and bloom and fade, like the swift passage of seasons. But you, O God, are from forever to forever. And we are made for you and for you alone. I come back to my desk third period, and there is the phrase from Merton that has come to mean so much to me: "The only true joy on earth is to escape from the prison of our own false self and to enter by love into union with the life who dwells and sings within the essence of every creature and in the core of our own souls."

And so "this bi-polar thing" goes on throughout the year. Images gradually crystalize to describe the process within. A favorite one is the gaudily colored hot air balloon tethered to earth by ropes unable to soar. The crew boss comes along with sharp axe and one by one severs the ropes that bind it to earth. There, one final rope is parted, and the balloon rises into the sky and heads over the countryside, past lakes and hills, free as a mystic, with the earth below a patchwork of beauty and the horizon to the west clean and clear and inviting.

The other image is the great eagle with banded leg chained to a low perch, unable to soar, yearning for the heights, yet earthbound, held in bondage. The liberator comes and severs the cord. The eagle stretches, opens his wings, and in widening circles arcs higher and higher, catches a thermal and with wings poised rises and soars.

# 12

## 1984, A Special Summer

### Calling in the Wilderness

It's suddenly the end of the year, graduation, goodbyes and two days later I'm entering retreat at Oshkosh retreat house. My retreat master of choice this year is Bob Leiweke, S.J., a spiritual director of much experience, a good friend, a small man, but direct and frank and fearless. Bob set me to work in our first short session praying over Jesus going out in the desert after his baptism.

I settled into chapel and re-created the Lord's experience as best I could. I asked him to let me know what it was like out in that desert solitude. How did it feel to leave behind the crowds and the rush of life and to experience the dead quiet of a desert night, the barren wilderness all around him, and the silent parade of stars above him. How he felt his soul moving out to his Father, the great God of the stars, and hearing again and again the words uttered in his depths, "My son, my beloved son, that's who you are. On you my favor rests." I let that scene and those words sink into my spirit in the quiet chapel.

Then after a long time, I went for a walk outside near the lake. The joy of a spring night, the cool wind rustling the waves, the lights of the city winking across the water. A sense of God came about me, not of him becoming present to me, but of me walking in him as in an all enveloping atmosphere. In him I live and move and have my being and walk this night, I in him, he present in the depths of my soul, the God of my life, as Guest. It was such a gentle sense of this God. I looked up into the sky at the Big Dipper, at Cassiopeia on the horizon, at the Milky Way band across the heavens, and then awoke with the sudden realization that these are the very same stars Jesus saw 2,000 years ago in the desert. He and I both look upon the same silent star show wheeling above, and each of us was deeply moved toward the Father. For a long time I prayed to the Lord that I might value solitude and stillness and seek it, might abandon rush and restlessness and spinning my wheels, might be rid of wearying chatter and endless yakking about trivia in the name of interpersonal relationship. I prayed to the Lord that I might share more deeply his own deep movement to his Father, the very source of his life. "You alone, God, you alone," the central quest of my life at last, after all these years of wandering and dead ends. I prayed for an abiding sense of the Lord's presence and thanked him for this evening by his side.

Strange, a remark of friend Jim Ryan, S.J., came to mind. A young scholastic trying to decide to stay or leave the order asked Jim how he coped with loneliness in Jesuit life. Jim's answer was simple and direct: "My answer to loneliness is prayer; I take it to God." Yes, God alone, the very source of my life.

The next morning Bob and I get together. I explain the movement of my prayer the day before. I tell him about the constantly recurring bi-polar movement in my life of light and shadow, darkness and drawing, frustration and desire for God alone. A bit haltingly, I speak of my feeling somewhat guilty living in this community of workaholics, in a high-energy youth culture where the premium is on being with it, in the flow of activity, alert to the latest of things and expressions, floating in a tide of conversations, meetings, parties and social events. Of how I feel leaving a whirlwind of active work in early afternoon for the luxury of some time apart, in stillness, biking alone, reading in areas that deeply nourish me, writing my journal. Of how I feel somehow unfaithful to those people who burn their energy out day after day in full teaching and activity schedules and endless curriculum meetings. And yet of how I feel drawn in my fifty-ninth year to shelve time, to make God and inner depth the great quest of my life these last years.

Bob listens carefully. Then with great clarity and deliberateness, he says, "John, go with it. You have an authentic call to the Lord. I set my seal on it: mystical. Don't be afraid of that word at all. If it worries you, use the word "experiential," because that's the way the Lord is leading you. What I hear in you is a deep cry for God. God is there within you, all about you. And he knows you through and through. He cares for you deeply. So go that route with gladness, not looking back."

I return to my room in vast peace. Yes, I see it again; basically over the years there's a consistency running through my life. Something is being done in me that even my own foolishness and infidelity cannot undo, like a strong current bearing me on. I spend the day with the simple mantra suggested by Bob, a cry of the heart: "Lord, come and save me." From my own mess inside, my weakness, my boredom, my angers, my negativity. "Lord, come and transform this mess into a new creature." Again I rediscover the Moses approach to prayer: "John, John." "Yes, Lord, here I am." "John, take off your shoes, you're standing on holy ground." Who are you, Lord?" "I am the God of Abraham and Moses and Isaiah and Jesus and Mary and Augus-tine and Francis and Ignatius and Damien and Helder Camara and Dorothy Day and young Peter and Tom, and I'm your God." Again it's a way of entering God's presence to start prayer.

Suddenly the morning Office becomes alive, swarming with individual lines that speak to my soul: "My heart and my flesh rejoice in the living God; I will pour water upon the thirsty land; I'll pour out my spirit and you'll grow like willows by flowing streams." On and on as I walk along Lake Winnebago, the image of lake and ocean water speaks to me. Winnebago in a storm is violent; waves churn and run and crash the rocky shore. But only the top three or four feet are disturbed. But down into the solemn green depths of Lake Superior or the Pacific Ocean the stillness and quiet reign. Yet even there, in the depths, the silent Japanese current runs. This image resonates. In this retreat to go with that depth movement, to be like the flat stone flung by a kid onto the water which skips twice, three times, and then sinks soundless into the green depths to find its home.

Two days later, after much listening, Bob said very deliberately, "John, what's going on in your life is basically the Third and Fourth weeks of the Spiritual Exercises. I mean your sharing in the suffering and death of Jesus. A process of dying to your old ways of going about things, to the activities of a lifetime, to your successes, to your impatient desires to achieve, to your selfish self that is being steadily eroded and purified by the Lord. And a sharing in the new way of living in the Risen Lord, in the new life being born in you, in God who is taking over more. Explore this new creation with the Lord. He is inviting you to himself. Let the past and its old ways go; move in joy into this new life, thirsting for him; let him do what he wants, when he wants. It's all in his hands."

A strong statement said with great emphasis by this small man of God. So much to ponder and assimilate. So much to wonder at. A new way of seeing the process of my life with its darkness and frustrations these last years.

The next day desire returns once more to finish writing that journal, to sing God's song in me, explore his gifts and praise him. It dawns on me all over again that I'm a person to whom God has given much, one blessed so deeply by God, one who has much to thank God for. He who is mighty has done great things for me. And holy is his name.

That afternoon, as clouds from a storm pulled off, I biked to my favorite pasture, wandered through green fields enjoying every moment, waded the creek, spread my blanket, knelt down in the grass, prostrated myself and adored God all about me; I lay there spread-eagled in the open sunshine, asking this God to come into me and fill my life. And life again was spontaneous, open and free before the rich sky of spring. I ran through the pasture exulting in my knee, strong once again, and then settled down in great peace to read Luke.

After dinner I boarded my bike again and, to the music of Talbot's "Magnificat," biked into a stunning evening. Fresh, clear, cool, the rich green of Wisconsin farmland all around me, the black earth newly plowed and glistening in the sunset rays, lilacs and apple in full blossom by road sides, the sun sinking in crisp glory. A world charged with God's grandeur. What I must do from here on is to live the present moment just as it is and enjoy it as it comes from the hands of God himself, an unrepeatable unique event to be taken, treasured, enjoyed and then let go. Contemplation, the long loving look at the real. God in the now. And so to forget the prospects of the ambitious self, the process the selfish self fancies. To let go and simply be with God in the now!

That night before bed these words from Abraham Heschel's great book, *I Asked for Wonder*, stopped my clock: "The issue of prayer is not prayer; the issue of prayer is God." And "It is gratefulness that makes the soul great." And "to join the movement towards him which surges unnoticed throughout the whole universe." This last statement haunts me.

It's May 30, and I get up early and go into the chapel and open up the baptism story. I picture the thirty-year-old carpenter going down into the brown water of the Jordan; John pushes his head under the water; Jesus comes up, water streaming off his hair, and then goes aside to pray. The heavens seem to open without warning, "torn apart" as Mark would call it; the Holy Spirit descends on Jesus and invades his conscious psychological life, touching him strongly. Jesus becomes alert, his whole soul quivering with God, his spirit wheeling out in desire to his Father. This, the landmark experience in Jesus' life, the moment of presence, of new identity.

I think to myself of my own history. For me at age fourteen on an April day at Campion; for me at age forty-six at John's tomb. The landmark moments when God moved into my conscious life to claim me. Then the awakening call at which my true self springs into existence. I taste that moment this morning with Jesus. To value that unforgettable moment, to live in fidelity to it.

Then Jesus hears the words he will never forget: "You are my Son, my beloved one, my favor rests on you." To know that he is special, not just another carpenter from a small town but the Son, the Beloved Son of God, the one whom God loves so specially.

I reflect on myself. The great phrases of Scripture come flooding back, ones that registered over and over, ones that I had chosen from the floor in CLC retreats.

"You didn't choose me John, I chose you": the scripture passage of my twenty-fifth anniversary year as a priest. "You are precious to me, John, the apple of my eye. You are mine. I will never let you go; I have loved you with an everlasting love. You are my beloved, I am the bridegroom; not because of any merit on your part; worthiness is not a category with me. I loved you and chose you before you were born. I first loved you, John."

Attracted by my emptiness, by my own inner poverty, my loneliness, my needing everything, my longing, he comes to me in my personal history time after time awakening my conscious life, claiming and capturing me forever by strong religious experience. And so he keeps telling me again and again what he told Jesus that day at the Jordan: you are my beloved Son and I love you.

Then I watch Jesus, *driven* by the Holy Spirit, deliberately severing all ties with people around him, heading out to the desert, craving the solitude he needs to be alone with God his Father, to savor the words he has heard in his depths, to ponder his new identity and how he will live with it and incorporate it.

I ponder my own call to growing solitude in the midst of an active life as teacher, of my own growing new identity and how I'm to live with it and experience it. With a good deal of wonder, I ponder all I share with the Eucharistic Christ.

All this before breakfast! Too much.

That day Bob says again with great clarity, striking the table with his fist: "By damn, John this is your call, the way God is calling *you*. Pray for a deepening of this love, yes, savor the present moment where God is. Indulge the contemplative in you, surrender to it; let it be, search for God. Surely, a balance must be kept between active and contemplative in your life, but do it."

Then he states something that I will ponder for years; he says it very deliberately. I ask him to repeat so that I can write it down. "John, the heart of it is this: to make the Lord and his immense love for you constitutive of your personal worth. Define yourself radically as one beloved by God; God's love for you and his choice of you constitute your worth. Accept that, and let it become the most important thing in your life."

We discuss it. The basis of my personal worth is not my possessions, my talent, not esteem of others, reputation, not high marks from provincial or superior or principal or department head, not kudos of appreciation from parents and kids, not applause, and everything telling you how important you are to the place. Rather a healthy, joyful freedom, a true independence from fickle, ill-informed judgments of people around you. I stand anchored now in God before whom I stand naked, this God who tells me "You are my son, my beloved one."

On Ascension Thursday, I wake up relaxed, deliciously rested, the best sleep in months. For the morning prayer, I go to a prayer form I've often used, an interchange of letters with God. Putting myself in his presence again, I write the Lord's sentiments to me at this moment, letting the pen go and the spirit express the Lord's feelings and desires for me. Only after the Lord's letter is completed do I respond with my own letter to the Lord. I'm deeply moved as I write; the sentences flow easily.

Dear John,

John, you are mine. Out of love I created you fifty-eight years ago; with care I fashioned your unique self; I sent you to that home in that Wisconsin River village to be formed and nurtured in faith. With a loving providence I've worked with your freedom over many years to bring you to this moment. I chose you out of many to be my own, my intimate. And so I broke into your life as a boy to attract you to myself alone, to make you mine. Time and time again I drew you to myself. In Rome, I came to you specifically to start the second deeper journey, the call within a call. In 1973 in the great retreat I revealed to you my ever-lasting love for you in a way you could not miss. In Guatemala, I came to you in the disguise of the poor and oppressed people of the world and touched your life. In these last four retreats, I've called you to myself in an unmistakable way. I've given you an authentic call to my very person. So come, John, my beloved son, come to the living waters. Satisfy your thirst, don't waste your life on what is useless. Come.

With Love,
Your God, the Beloved

Then my letter that flowed easily and with such joy.

Dear God,
I stand here before you, my great God: Good Father, Bridegroom, Living Spirit, Great Trinity, the Beloved Guest. I am
yours; you call me, as I am, to yourself. I want to seek you
with all my heart this coming year, you alone, God, you
alone. Let me not be afraid of solitude, of aloneness; instead
let me seek it. Lord, my deepest identity is this: I am an
emptiness longing for your fullness, a poverty longing for
your richness, a capacity created for you alone. You look on
me and say: John, you are my beloved one, my special Son;
and, Lord, that is enough for me. This is what constitutes my
inner worth. I want to stand in your sight, own what I am and
be free of all human opinion and judgment. I am what I am,
one loved by God lavishly in a life history. Help me this year
to walk my own way, loving you and serving you, bringing
you to those to whom you send me, to build your world in
justice and peace and to do it your way. Help me keep on
loving others even when there's no return at all, as you did.
Lord, continue to draw me to yourself.
With Love,<br>John

## The Lesson of Yosemite

Twelve days later, I fly to San Francisco for a religious
education workshop for theology teachers in Jesuit schools at
Santa Clara University. But first, two days of sight-seeing in San
Francisco and then a bus to Yosemite Valley, one of my favorite
places on God's earth. It's a deep valley seven miles long, one
mile wide, the heart of the Sierra Nevada mountains. Sheer
granite walls tower up 3,000 feet from the valley floor and great
waterfalls like Bridal Veil and Yosemite and Snow Bird fall
from the heights to the Merced River below. The winter has
been snowy, so the waterfalls are roaring at full volume. I've
scheduled four days of hiking and want to test my years and my
knee with good long climbs.

I had earlier decided, after good contemplative times biking and cross-country skiing alone, that I would climb alone in

Yosemite and Glacier Park, following the urge to solitude the Lord had planted in me. My first evening I borrow a bike from Tony Huffman, a child-psychologist working at the lodge for the summer, and take a leisurely fourteen-mile tour of the valley's grandeur once again, lingering at the base of Half Dome and Bridal Veil. Then back to my tent cabin where I pull down Harvey Egan's *Christian Mysticism*, the key book I'll spend the summer on.

The next morning I pull on my hiking boots and walk fourteen miles in the sunshine, climbing 6,000 feet on my favorite trail. I climb out of the valley via the steep "Mist Trail" alongside the Merced River to Vernal Falls, thundering 300 feet to the rocks below. Then past exuberant waterwheel rapids up a steep rock trail along the left side of Nevada Falls, dropping 500 feet in full glory. There, on the porch above the falls, I have lunch. In the afternoon I climb higher and higher along the Panorama Trail with Nevada Falls below, Half Dome towering to the north, the sharp decline of the valley to the right. Down a bit to Alouette Falls and a sponge-off in the ice-cold water and relief for hot, tired feet. Two more miles through rich forest and I break out on Glacier Point where the cliffs drop a sheer 3,000 feet to the valley floor. The view in every direction is glorious. A sandwich dinner there. Then more hiking to my sunset spot, Sentinel Dome, the highest point in the area, bare granite surrounded by Jeffrey pine, with a 360-degree view of high Sierra country, waterfalls and all. The sunset comes gradually and gently, long shadows creep up the canyons, and the after-glow lingers. At length I head home and hitchhike my way twenty-eight miles to my cabin.

The next day I reverse the process: hitchhike to the heights and then walk mostly downhill all day to the valley, linger where I want, capturing the best in Fujicolor.

During these four days of hiking alone, I'm slowly growing conscious of an inner process that parallels my outer mountain climbing journey. This is how I experience it and the contem-plative things I've learned.

At first my mind was preoccupied with details of the journey, with worries about leaving things behind, with plans not yet crystalized. As I climbed, old anger surfaced and subsided, an unpleasant set of experiences that soured my last visit here, things people said the last year, unpleasant circumstances in my community, the whole web of frustration of goals. As the morning went on, these specters rose before me, troubling my surface, and then dropped away, one by one. Consciously at one point I did the familiar routine: facing the old complexities, the sadnesses, absurdities, and turning my back on them. Let the dead bury the dead; the past is past. Future uncertainties about details and health I put deliberately in the hands of a loving Providence. Lord, your will be done. All will work out.

I began to concentrate on the simple elemental joy of hiking. The exuberance and freshness at the beginning, the basic experience of body functioning, one foot in front of the other for hours, ten to twelve miles worth, gentle downgrades through rich cool forest, sweating up the long switchbacks in the open sun, feeling leg muscles and back muscles going sore one by one, the crush of shoes and granite gravel and the start of a heel blister, getting into stride and loosening up and feeling good. Moments of weakness in the morning but an infusion of steady energy in the afternoon, all the way to the top of the Panorama; then sponging off sitting in the cool stream and the push to the top. Thoughts stop, feelings purify, one concentrates on the elemental work of the hiker, breathing from the depths of the lungs, feeling the heart beat fast and sure in high elevation, experiencing tension depart and looseness all over, and the knowledge that at fifty-eight all still works well indeed. So good to get in touch with this again, and to do it with enthusiasm.

Then a further stage: to center on the present moment alone as though there were no other; to take each moment and live it fully, to be aware, as much as possible, of each breath, of heart beating, of life gladly possessed, to be aware of one's next step, to place it clearly; to see sunlight and cloud and shadow and the play of the rainbow in waterfall and the exuberant joy of fast-running mountain water. To achieve as complete awareness as possible; to see, to contemplate each thing, and to see it anew. Selfless climbing. And in that heightened awareness, somehow, by gift, by deep intuition, to sense the Lord in each breath and each heart beat, the Lord at play, dancing with his creation.

A third process which I became painfully aware of: that first day, I was conscious that this might be my last time in this valley I so loved. So I felt I had to catch and freeze in picture the beauty unrolling before me on the Panorama Trail. I found myself snapping picture after picture almost compulsively. I had to see it all, every trail, to capture it all in ultimate photographs and so freeze it forever, to possess it. This put a pressure on me, a hurry, a compulsion. Suddenly I brought myself up short. No, learn this once and for all. You can't possess anything; you can't really hold anything in nature, in friendship, in beauty. It's all transient, passing, in a flow past you. Only God remains and he will be forever. As C.S. Lewis tells the photographer at the end of *The Great Divorce,* "Come and see; he is endless." So yes, see all these great sights. In freedom take fine pictures, but never try to possess and hold. Be free, enjoy the moment, and let it go. Let Nevada Falls go, let Vernal Falls go, let Half Dome go, let sunset on Sentinel go. Eat at the banquet of life with detachment. In the next life you'll possess immortal beauty, God forever, and you will absorb it and be absorbed by him.

Now it comes clear to me that hiking too is a grand paradigm for living. Basically I'm a traveler, a journeyer through life to the great vision at the end. All else I encounter other than God is not God. More like individual pieces of a broken mirror that reflect, however imperfectly, God who is beauty himself. Yes, these individual pieces of the mirror catch and hold and haunt you. But you were made for God alone. I'm a traveler to the dawn.

## God's Continuous Presence

The next week finds me at Santa Clara for the religious ed workshop for eighty Jesuit high school theology teachers. From the first day, despite the poor presentations, I experienced an unmistakable palpable presence of God. I could turn within when-ever I wanted to and find it. The image that catches it best is a quiet pilot light on a gas stove always burning, like a little candle or lamp wick in a dark room, delicately flickering at any movement of air, easily blown out, easily ignored by brighter lights, yet burning with a quiet determination of its own. You God, Father, Son, Holy Spirit, dwelling palpably in my depths!

While biking I seem best able to tune in. But as many a class that week drones on interminably, I simply dive into my depths where the Lord awaits me with the mantra "You, Lord, you alone," and again I'm in the Lord's green pastures. This phenomenon continues for two and a half weeks. The presence of God is no longer a practice I work at, but a perceptible reality I live in daily, a given, nothing that I do but which just happens. Then, as suddenly as it began, the feeling of God's presence ceases. I wonder at this.

In the next two weeks, as I worked my way to Ignatius, Montana, I experienced three moments of almost unbearable beauty and wonder that linger still in memory: running freely and joyfully along the edge of crashing surf on a long, lovely deserted Pacific Ocean beach strewn with logs and driftwood; a late night walk alone amid towering redwood trees south of Leggett with moonlight softly filtering through the trees; and a fourteen-mile hike along the Pacific Crest Trail to a snow-clogged ledge at the foot of towering 12,000 foot Mt. Adams with former student, camper, and skier friend, Mark Pilliod. This last was climaxed by a quiet Mass back at our tent site with Mt. Adams soaring to the east bathed in pink alpine glow. After communion Mark and I split for a half hour of prayer. I walked up a fire road to a cliff opposite, and there suddenly all the trees on my left turned silver. Surprised, I turned to the southeast and saw the rising full moon drenching the front of Mt. Adams in mist. The heart-stopping beauty of that privileged moment.

## Two Prayer Days on the Mountain

It's St. Ignatius Day, July 31, and I'm doing weekend help at St. Ignatius Mission, Montana, a pilgrimage place for me.

After four days of intensive hiking on major trails the week before, I plan to celebrate Ignatius day with an afternoon of prayer above Logan Pass going over the insights and special moments of my June retreat. So I drive the Going-to-the-Sun Highway past Bird Woman Falls up to the Logan Pass, park, and then hike a couple thousand feet higher to an open saddle ablaze with a profusion of flowers between the two Matterhorn-like mountains, Clements and Reynolds. I'm 7,000 feet up abreast the Continental Divide, looking down on blue-green Hidden Lake. A magnificent cirque of mountains surrounds the lake and rises from my left to snow-clad peaks and glaciers in the south and to snow-streaked Bearhat Mountain soaring up from the western shore. Four great terraces of rock with many waterfalls drop precipitously to the lake.

I take my perch on the second terrace on a rock crag overlooking the shimmering lake. There at noon I spread my retreat notes, my sandwich and oranges, camera, knapsack and Walkman and begin a blessed afternoon with the great music of the ages. I put on Mozart, Beethoven, "Les Preludes," and settle down in this grandest of spots to a contemplative day. My friends Hector and George, two white mountain goats that roam the pass, come and graze close by, quite at home with me. When it gets hot in the afternoon sun, I drop down one level and cool off under a waterfall spilling off the cliff from the snows above. My effort in this prayer day is to try to crystalize the key insights and graces of my June retreat, to unwrap God's graces to me and savor them and so let them sink deep roots in me. Basically, it's a way of thanking God for his gifts.

Around 3:30 I decide to take a break for awhile, so I get up and walk north to the foot of Clements Mountain where white mountain goats are frolicking. I hike along in the warm sun fascinated by the goats at play. Then a honeymoon couple so obviously in love come, arms intertwined, enjoying every moment of the walk together. Overcome by the beauty of it all, they stop at a ledge and kiss.

Suddenly it hits me, an old insight become new again: the separate vocation of celibacy, the whole different way that I'm called to. God alone is my portion, my prize, my eternal partner. He is my one heart's love. He is my intimate and no one else. My best times I share with him as well as my worst. My happiness is with him. God alone. As a husband gives his life for better or for worse, so I give my life for better or worse to my

God. There this couple enjoy the beauty of a summer afternoon on the Pass with each other, here I am enjoying it with my God.

Two separate calls. Two ways to God. Let me walk my life and live my commitment to God all the way to the end as I vowed so long ago. I'm married to my God. He is the deepest companion of my soul. God my wife! My eternal partner, my intimate, my beloved one. And this, the deepest rationale for celibacy, the deepest cure for the heart's loneliness, the ultimate answer to no family, to no children, to no grandchildren, to no deeply affective climate about me. The answer is God alone. He is my portion. My soul belongs to somebody else.

The sudden rush of this insight took my breath away, and there up on the Divide my spirit took wing again and exulted in the Lord. With great joy I went back to my perch, surveyed the mountain scene and settled back into my retreat notes. A blessed time that filled me with the Lord.

The next day, August 1, I decided on another prayer day on the Divide. This time I chose the skyline trail. Picture the scene. I began on the top of the Divide. At the start the path is three or four feet wide, cut into a sheer granite cliff for some 800 feet, with rope for the fearful to grasp. Then I walked for about five miles with the great spiny rocks of the Divide rising up sheer 1,000 feet into the sky on my right. To my left, meadow green and forest sloped steeply away till the drop was 2,000 feet to the roadway and gorge below. Bear grass, Indian paint-brush, and a myriad other flowers were everywhere. Ahead were range after range of snow-clad mountains disappearing into Canada. Across the valley to my left great mountain slopes mantled in green soared right up to the glacier and high peaks. Lovely Bird Woman Falls cascaded in splendor from the glaciers into a green lake. This stunning scene unrolled as I walked the roof of the world with the music of Beethoven and Zamfir and Mozart in my ears. Finally, near Haystack Rock, I found my place, down from the trail on a crag near an old twisted tree. I spent the day there reflecting on the awesomeness of God in all things, a favorite realization that Merton often wrote of: awareness as a way of seeing, an insight into the deepest reality of things; to see and to know that the whole universe is an embodiment of God's love, an enfleshing of his creating word, a moving, breathing sacrament of God.

All creation is word of God. This immense God before all time, before anything else was, before Pre-Cambrian mountains, before solar systems and universes, before "Big Bang," before matter, this immense Lord-thought universe, thought planets, thought life, thought man and woman. Then he uttered his creation word and a universe streamed into existence. His knowing me and uttering me causes me to be. And so the whole universe is the word of God, an embodiment of his creative love, his sacrament. And I am a word of God enfleshing his love.

Radical awareness of what-is may seem a simple thing, yet it is a gift of God given when asked for. The whole point of living is finally to unwrap the package of life and to discover this God in my depths and in the depths of the world about me. To learn to see what is at the heart of all life, what lies as close to me as my next breath and my next heartbeat, the bear grass just off the trail or the Indian paint brush at my feet or the mountains just up the trail.

That whole day I spend on the rim of the world entertaining that one insight, enjoying it, returning to it, living in God's presence high up on my perch.

# 13

# The Next Two Years

## The Bi-polar Movement Deepens

In moments of insight, I glimpse that what is going on in me is a purification of my radical self-centeredness, the fixed sense of my own importance, me the hub of the wheel, me a special person important to many. All of this is being cut away, stroke by stroke, by the action of life itself. Self is being burnt out so that one thing alone remains, the me, poor in spirit, me needing God and thirsting for him alone, and God enthroned at last in the temple of my heart with all idols destroyed and a heart of flesh compassionate and warm with outgoing love.

In retrospect, I can name exactly how that purification is being worked in me. The sense of vital energy and health ebbing, of older age coming. I think I've got the diabetes controlled perfectly, but then blood sugar soars once in November '85, then again in March '86 to 300, with deep fatigue and a flood of baffling symptoms that send me scurrying to doctor and dietician. Puzzling, depressing times. Skin cancer breaking out on my face, surgery needed on the top of my head for it, two further flareups on my back. And then one day in April '86, I lose the remaining upper teeth in my mouth and endure a month and more of pain and discomfort on a bread and soup diet while dentures adjust to my mouth. What dentures do to me symbolically and how they distort my face make public speaking appearances and eating difficult. Biting into sweet corn and apples and other food becomes impossible, and they're put behind. My hearing begins to fade, and I can't follow conversations and have to ask embarrassingly to repeat words. The tension from the wear and tear of classroom life with messy teenagers becomes more of a reality.

The daily joy I have in contact with young people slowly fades, and I wonder at this disappearance. Teaching teenagers becomes more and more of a chore, often a bore. I feel my best and deepest currents are unused, underutilized with people too young to understand. I drop CLC work with the young. Disciplinary situations where I'm challenged by the balkiness or resistance of the adolescent trouble me and warp my teaching if I'm not careful. I inwardly feel that I'm regarded by a number of the young as just another older teacher somewhat out of it, and I hate the knowing, condescending smile some flash at me.

The Third World thing, triggered by experience of the world's poor in '74, deepened by ten years of analysis and implementation, glows in me; I want to communicate it to the kids I teach. But I'm living in Reaganland where the median income of our parents is $58,000, an upper-middle-class milieu increasingly resistant to challenges, settling down into the apathy and job security of the 1980s. Whenever I try to communicate what glows in me, it turns my Jesuit friends and students off. My Jesuit brothers criticize what I do as negative and inappropriate developmentally. The return to questions on world hunger, on systematic structure in El Salvador and Nicaragua, on Star Wars and MX and B1 and arms control: dead silence and people pull away.

Now I feel a sense of desolation whenever I touch these great issues of our times, a helplessness to address them effectively in this alien milieu. Was it a ten-year waste, all this work? Frustration is keen in my course on the arms race and the American bishops' peace pastoral and the Bread for the World homeroom. My dissatisfaction with the Order I love and its higher superiors and their response goes on but is more and more muted. I watch us turn inward to worrying about vocations, to caring for retirement and an aging constituency, to making our communities more comfortable and to pulling subtly away from the General Congregation's commitment to solidarity with the poor and to challenging a warlike, consuming society. My advice is no longer sought or desired. I am simply out of step. The abyss widens; I sense something precious is dying before my eyes.

Community life becomes difficult for me. Thirty-eight men living closely together, with outer civility and tolerance certainly, has an impersonalness about it that increasingly gets to me. A cultivated anonymity with little sharing of the inner deep currents of our Jesuit life, the richness within which I long to share and for which I entered religious life. Instead so many conversations about computers and Packers and Warriors and kids and dances and sports and our work. Chatter that leaves me empty inside. I guess the thing that hits me most is the sense of being passed over in this fine community, of being regarded as a has-been, a person not worth cultivating by young Jesuits or even by people my own age. The deepest things in me I cannot adequately share; it's as though few are even interested in joining me on my journey.

Yes, these, some obvious, some subtle, are the major difficulties I'm going through. Yet when I feel the touch of frustration, of a sense of uselessness, of moments of sadness, growing isolation, I have the inner sense becoming more and more clear that this is God's touch in my life, his burning coal purifying all else in me, doing-in my dogged sense of self-importance, destroying it finally bit by bit, and in the middle of it all, calling me to himself more deeply. Yes, God, you alone.

Yet this dark side is only one side of the movement. Time after time the Lord surprises me with quiet invasions of his presence, in-depth invitations to himself. One Saturday morning lying in bed, I feel this simple desire for the Lord welling up in my depth like a pure spring of water. The wanting him and him alone and to give myself to him flames out more and more and grows and grows, not with emotional intensity, but gently from my depths, a simple, pure uncomplicated spring bubbling up to conscious life. My mind and heart are clear and uncluttered, utterly attentive to the Spirit breathing within me, creating desire I feel impossible to express in words. The presence of God, not something I do, but something that happens to me.

There were many other privileged moments: times at
Sunday Mass in my parish where we hold hands at the Our
Father and sing our hearts to the Lord and I'm so moved;
breathtaking moments skiing in the Porkies in a snowstorm
when there's a sense of God everywhere in the storm and the
trees and in my heart; moments in the classroom where I turn
seniors on to mystics like Merton and Hammarskjold and
sparks fly; deeply moving counselling sessions; marvelous
conversations with people who feel a similar pull to God in
their depths.

A number of books over these two years illumined my path
and nourished me. Abraham Heschel, the Hasidic Jewish mystic
and social prophet, comes streaming into my life through a
book of his quotes, *The Wisdom of Heschel* by Ruth Goodhill.
Heschel explores in-depth privileged moments in the life of
every human that contain the transcendental God: experiences
of awe, the sublime, of wonder, of radical amazement. Many of
his lines enter into my soul. A companion for the journey. For
example: "We dwell on the edge of mystery and ignore it,
wasting our souls, risking our stake in God." "To pray is to
regain a sense of the mystery that animates all beings. ... Prayer
is our humble answer to the inconceivable surprise of living."
"Faith is not the clinging to a shrine but an endless pilgrimage
of the heart." "God is of no importance unless he is of supreme
importance."

Other books I devour: William Johnson's *Christian Mysticism
Today* and its emphasis on the sacramental principle; Nouwen's
*Letters from the Genesee*, a favorite I return to yearly; finally
Rahner's little gem *I Remember* with preface by Harvey Egan,
S.J., which gives me the theological foundation I desire. Rahner
is convinced that at the root of everyone's existence is a core
mystical experience of God, a basic intentional thing in one's
depths, a mystery that haunts every human heart. We may
deny and repress it, ignore and snow it under, but it is the
deepest reality of our lives and provides the horizon of each life.
Egan assures me that this pervades every page of Rahner's
works and is the linchpin of his theological thought. This
squares with my own experience and becomes my approach
with others.

Such books are companionship on a mysterious way, friends who meet you at dark intersections and who light up your life, buoyant travelers who call you to step out on the mountain trail, who give confidence and encouragement and inspiration on the journey. I search for such.

An unusual thing happens in March. I'm asked to direct a talented sister from rural Brazil to help her discern her future course. I'm busy, have no time to reflect deeply or to pray at length, but the eight days together are grace-filled. I find myself saying things that seem so clear and sure, proposing movements that turn out to be just right for her. Scripture passages float up unbidden which the Lord uses to bring about marvelous peace and closeness to himself. I'm overwhelmed by what happens in these eight days, as though the Lord used me and my poverty to do just what he wanted for her. We marvel together at the work of the Holy Spirit. For this one event alone, if for no other reason, I feel that the whole Third World experience in Guatemala and its consequent difficulties was all supremely worthwhile, if only God could finally use it to help Darlene.

## 1985 Retreat and Final Closure

Retreat in 1985 was a mingled event. Two very significant things occurred. On the third day my director suggested Mark 14: 3-10, the story of the woman who broke the jar of precious ointment and poured the costly perfume over Jesus' head. The Apostles' reaction was immediate. "Why this waste? The money could have been used to feed the poor." Judas and Peter and James and John condemn her. But Jesus' eyes blaze and he defends her, stopping them short.

Now leave her alone; why do you upset her! She has done a good work. The poor you'll always have with you and you can help them whenever you wish, but you won't always have me with you. She did all she humanly could for me and it is good. ... And I tell you this solemnly, wherever my gospel is preached, I want you to tell her story.

I spent the day before the Blessed Sacrament or walking outside, taking part in this scene and hearing our Lord's words. Suddenly each part of this incident came alive and spoke directly to me and to my experience.

"This waste." The contemplative task, spending more time alone with God, seeking him more now in solitude, seeking awareness of this God who comes subtly into my life, when the cosmic dance beats in my every breath and heartbeat, you, God, you alone, to praise you, to sit in your presence just being with you, following this deep bent in my bones, writing of God's gifts to me, celebrating them, exploring them, capturing them in words, living in thanks: this the great work of my fifties and sixties—writing and biking contemplatively and saving space for God.

For years I've been immersed in a blizzard of activities, and now I want slowly to cut back to where I can authentically live and follow deeper bents. Yet I feel a sense of guilt, that I'm not, after twenty-five years, pulling my share. Cultivating this deeper awareness of God and his presence seems an illusion. Am I fooling myself? Isn't it nonproductive? Yet it is deeply nourishing. But I can't explain it to anybody. Lord, you've put me in a solitude, and no one will ever know.

"Now leave her alone." Jesus speaks to me clearly, authoritatively. "Leave him alone, alone with me. Let him squander this time on me, lavishly pouring it out on me and on contemplative awareness and following the deep pull of his inner life. Let him seek me with all his heart. He is doing a good work; let him do it. Leave him free to lavish his attention on me and me alone. Let him go the way I'm calling him; you people go the way I'm calling you."

"The poor you will always have with you." Yes, El Salvador, Guatemala, Nicaragua, Ethiopia, and Bangladesh will be there, always hurting, oppressed, stifled by terribly unjust structures, and this for the foreseeable future. Yes, we will be locked in an intolerable arms race jockeying for world power, massive expenditures while the world's hungry go without. This seems to be the reality of life that defies all attempt to remedy. You can get upset, angry, go into tirades, get chewed up with frustration, but to what avail? Yes, help where I can, but here and now I'm called to something deeper and so have a basic sense of freedom. Me you will not always have with you, so honor my presence, love me alone, pay attention to me, seek and cultivate this great presence. Mary did what was in her power, and this is all she could do. God's presence, his coming is in no way in my power. It is his gift completely. I in my depths am poor, empty, a sinner and that is my deepest truth. My place is to be attentive to him, to present myself in my poverty and open myself radically to him and his coming and respond to him.

"Wherever this Gospel is preached." I praise Mary. I want her story told wherever the Gospel is preached.

"So let her be." These words cut loose a whole burst of freedom in me. "Let John be. Let him center his life on me, vibrate with my presence, open up and out to the blue sky and the passage of clouds and soar with swallows and hawks, expand with starlight, glory in the wind and lightning and thunder, wonder at my presence in all that is, praise and glorify me, love me, feel desire for me, experience me, turn in to the gentle flame within where I dwell. Let him cultivate it all joyously and come to me."

And the flip side too: "Let him find me in the desert thirst, in the ache felt deep, the long loneliness, the tragic events and tragic sense in life, in the abyss that separates the human from his God, in the emptiness of the human heart made for God."

Let me be open to life as it comes in the present moment, in the cosmic dance, the river of joy just under the surface of life, open to God's presence and activity, to meet God in day-to-day life and say yes to him, to lavishly pour out the contents of my heart, to let the Lord play me like a musical instrument and, when he's done, drop me inert.

At last I determined to do final closure on a whole train of thoughts that have troubled me for years, closure on the whole Central American thing, the hunger and poverty thing, closure on the nuclear war and arms race thing, closure on the superiorship thing and on frustration with Jesuit renewal rhetoric. To put it all behind me. It's good I did what I did when I did it, but now it's no longer where I am. And so to go this new way that God is opening up for me, to follow his lead, to live in the present moment. I feel a great sense of freedom as though finally I'm breaking out into the clear like a broken-field runner finally emerging into the open.

On the sixth day of the retreat, my director encourages me to put myself before the Lord in the Blessed Sacrament and pose the question very personally to the Lord: "How do you, Lord, look at me? What do you feel in your heart for me?" Just sit there and pose that question and tune in to the mind and heart of Jesus, and let him answer it in his own good time and his own way. I spent much time on that sixth day before the Lord tapping into his inner life, going back to landmark words of his and letting them sink into my soul, pondering what he has done in me over the years.

That night I took a long leisurely bike ride across the green fields, watching the silent drama of sunset and cloud on a cool, crisp spring evening, and suddenly it all focused. The words of Elizabeth Barrett Browning's poem "How Do I Love Thee?" came to me, and it was as though Jesus went over with me the story of my life and "some of the ways" over the years with increasingly frequency and deeper emphasis that he kept saying "how I love you."

Long shadows deepen across freshly plowed fields as I ride on and the sunset goes grand. All of creation seems to speak to me. This great God of the sky and sunset and universe loves me. Joy breaks loose like sudden streams. And there forms in me what I can call only an *invincible certitude*; yes, those words are just right. The wonder of it all that the gracious coming of the Lord in my life should happen to me, and not once only but so often, and more steadily in the last five years, though more and more gently. These events I see clearly are God's touch, his kiss, his warm embrace, his making love to me and expressing the content of his heart. It's so very clear tonight. Lord, you can't make it much clearer.

This and this alone is the anchor of my self-worth. So I feel a calm freedom. Who the hell cares what others think of me, how they judge me? People will think what they want, judging from externals, but their judgments are their problem. I know who I am in the Lord. And so I shall walk the way the Lord leads me with peace and with joy. I'll try to radiate to my fellow

Jesuits and to students and parents and all I meet the Lord's warm, compassionate love. These insights fill my heart and mind as the sunset purples and I head my bike home. I'm filled with a sense of God's presence all about me, of joy and peace and love and I rest in invincible certitude. On my return I come into the Lord's presence in the chapel and thank him for telling me the content of his heart and ask that I may return again and again to tap into the richness of his inner life.

# 14

# 1986, My House Destroyed and Rebuilt

It's June 1986, and I'm making my eight-day retreat at the Jesuit Retreat house in Gloucester, Massachusetts, on a cape jutting out into the Atlantic. A world of ocean view and waves and granite rock and fog and lobster boats, a marvelous locale for a retreat. My retreat director is Sr. Joan McCarthy, who was strongly recommended by Bob Leiweke as just right for me. I approach our first session thinking I would spend twenty minutes or so, no more, cueing her into my present state of soul and a bit on my background. An hour and fifteen minutes later I came to a start realizing that the lunch period was fast disappearing. Each day thereafter we spent an hour and fifteen minutes regularly, and the time seemed all too short. So much was happening.

Joan listened to me very intently; what a gift to have someone join you so fully on your journey to God. She put her finger unerringly on the heart of the matter, expanding it with a short comment or further question. She gave me at the end of the first session three gospel passages for prayer; the first of these, the Martha-Mary story, I stayed with for eight days. It was an unfailing source of nourishment and grace, and I returned to it again and again. Joan's questions were penetrating and opened me to God: "When in the last twenty-four hours did you most feel God's presence?" "When our Lord spoke these words of Scripture to you, what was the look on his face? What was in his heart as he said this?" Such seemingly innocent questions focused me more completely on the Lord.

The first day I found myself tired and fatigued. So I slept it off and biked in glorious sunshine along Atlantic Avenue, sat by the Eastern Point lighthouse, walked the debris-laden beach, hunched down by the rocks watching a high tide crash in about me, slowly relaxing into the presence of God. Gradually I entered more and more on two realities: 1) this is the day the Lord has made, so let's rejoice and be glad in the only moment we have, the now; 2) to simply be with the Lord who indwells in me all day long. As Merton would say, "We already have what we seek within us, so no need to rush around to scurry elsewhere." Or as John Michael Talbot sings, "This is holy ground; we're standing on holy ground, for the Lord is present and where he is is holy." My prayer becomes a single turning inward, "You, God, you alone." Slowly the rush and disordered junk from my past, the accumulated rot of the year, recedes, the upset Martha in me, and I settle at Mary's side with the Lord, the one necessary thing in life.

Once again my surroundings begin to speak to me of God. I go out to read the Office in the morning, and sentences from the Psalms and Ignatius of Antioch and Bonaventure speak to my heart and give it wings. A simple walk along a beach with gulls shrieking overhead breathes God's presence in every part. Waves crash into the rocks and deep calls out to deep within me. Rain falls, four inches in the next few days, so I walk with an umbrella and contemplate and am endlessly filled with a gentle sense of the Lord all about and in me.

The eight days amaze me. So peacefully, so much is happening inside, almost too much. No desolation at all, or period of groping, or desert period of powerlessness and need. Only insight and deep attraction and light and calm. More is happening than I can take in. The contemplations I've so often made cease to be a mere exercise and become rather a reality I live and taste.

Joan tells me, "Look, John, you're finding God and experiencing him everywhere, in sunlight and rain, on the beach, in the ocean, in the Office and scripture, in your reading, in your inner self and your deep desires, in the memory of your past life, in the quiet before the Blessed Sacrament or riding your bike. It's the reality of the "Contemplation for Obtaining Divine Love" [the prayer which Ignatius gives as the last experience of a thirty-day retreat]. You're experiencing God present everywhere and working in you and in all creation." So she urges me to stay where I am and let the God whom I'm finding everywhere communicate freely with me. She tells me something I already know but need to hear again and again: "God desires to do so much more for you than you desire for yourself. So go with it, John. Trust your own experience. Relax more; there's no need to analyze what God's doing or try to manage it. What God wants most is your heart, John; ask him to reveal himself more in all that is." I go out from my conference and read a line from the Office that stops me cold: "You are my God; apart from you I have no good." Exactly.

I know instinctively this Sunday morning that the background to all this is Lorraine's statement in 1981: "John, you have an authentic call to the very person of God, God alone." And Bob Leiweke's statement in 1984: "John, two things are going on in you now: the third week of the Exercises, radical purification of your selfish self done by the Lord, your sharing in his passion; and the fourth week of the Exercises, his strong call and invitation to closer union with himself, your share in his resurrection."

Years ago and from time to time since, I've had intuitive glimpses of the vague thing that was coming: the whole somewhat false facade I had been going with, the house of my own that I had been erecting for years, a good house and yet a sense of something not quite right, something out of kilter, like a billiard ball that looks fine but wobbles when it rolls, something mine, not wholly his.

And suddenly the image of a house rose before me. For five days I had bicycled past three grand old three-story stone houses perched up on the rocks fronting the ocean. I saw the gleaming house that I painstakingly put together in my early Jesuit life and the early years of priesthood, that house that brought esteem and the sweet smell of external success and applause. I watched myself assemble that house. It began to take shape in 1950 at St. Louis U. High. Shaky and insecure, I plunged into teaching teenagers and suddenly there was success. I loved the kids, they loved me. I taught them English, coached their teams, led their sodality groups, counseled endlessly and made so many friends. I had found my life work, was effective, longed to do it the rest of my life; and the word on me was successful high school teacher, wonderful with youth.

Then the priesthood in 1956 and the boy priest syndrome and the spontaneous appreciation of people: first at the Indian government school, then at St. Francis Hospital, and then acceptance and acclaim at St. Paul Retreat House. I loved my priesthood for people, and they responded, and it was good. In the fall of '58, the whole package came together as the youth apostle settled in for first assignment at Marquette High. Senior English and theology teacher, counselor for so many who sought me out, heading the whole retreat program to the tune of nine closed retreats a year, building a strong CLC program on the foundation of the Exercises. I reveled in the contact with teenagers. I was well known now in the city's youth circles, esteemed for insight, sought out for retreats and talks, was a rallying point for young Jesuits whom I gladly recruited for CLC and counseling work. By March I'd be dealing with twenty-five seniors giving serious thought to the Society of Jesus and priesthood. And ten to fourteen a year would go regularly to the novitiate. The house was building more quickly.

Renewal on the wings of Vatican II broke out. I moved fully into that renewal: I took summer courses from the best around the country to renew myself: Häring and Brown, Sheets and Cooke, Quesnell and Baum. Gladly I jumped into Cursillo and Marriage Encounter and Better World Movement, riding the crest of renewal in the Church. People spoke of their admiration at my willingness to change and grow. The renewal whiz.

Suddenly one November, in the midst of a blizzard of activity, I'm invited to become rector of forty-two Jesuits at Marquette High. And for two years I do it. I seem to be on top of the world. The shiny, gleaming house is almost complete. One last step: I sign for Guatemala and love it and the next year am program director for Guatemala.

So now the house is in place, shiny and bright. I have applause and esteem. They congratulate me for my flexibility and leadership and enthusiasm and what I've done and am doing. But this house of mine is somehow askew: it's my house, not the Lord's house. "In vain do the builders build." And yet I know in my heart that each step was taken because it was right and seemed to be the Lord's way. Yes, it was, but he had something else in mind for it.

Then another image rose spontaneously as I walked along. It was the Lord as an artillery captain who came in front of my fine house dragging his cannon and proceeded deliberately and systematically to shoot the whole damn thing apart. Story by story, wall by wall, brick by brick he gunned down the house that took me twenty-five years to build until only rubble was left, pieces of masonry on the ground, and I'm standing there with the debris of my life at my feet looking at the ruins.

The strange thing was this big wide grin on the Lord's face as he gunned it apart in high glee. It's as though he said to me: now watch the top story while I blow it apart. There! Now watch the second story: there it goes! Isn't that great? Now watch the back wall: hooray! Now the side walls, now finally the front and it's all gone. Isn't that marvelous! And he turned to me with joy and warmth and smiled on me with much encouragement.

How did he do it step by step in my life history? First the superior's job became in my third year a nightmare. So much suffering in our men: for the first time I'm snagged in agonizing dilemmas, damned if you do, damned if you don't; increasingly I'm called to play God in the lives of others. Personal care exacts a terrible toll; I can't get to sleep until 3:00 A.M. I feel the deepest current in my life, being a high school teacher and pastoral person, being wrenched out of its course with increasing violence. After three years, I can't hack it any longer without cracking.

Shortly thereafter low-lying depression starts in an on-and-off basis. I feel my happiness and enthusiasm gone. The mask has been torn off; the Society of Jesus has been demythologized for me. I see us not as shining troops but as a suffering body, resistant to in-depth renewal and happy if a superior supplies a steady stream of conveniences. The throngs of young people who enter the Order leave in droves. Soon three rather than twelve enter the Jesuits from Marquette High, then none. The Church renewal I entered into so buoyantly goes into anger in 1968, then into ambiguity and excess and bewilderment. A curious backlash and suspicion springs up in the 70s. The tag "liberal" becomes suspect. Theologically we emphasize credibility with our clientele, but the heady enthusiasm of renewal gives way to a heaviness and to stridency and bewilderment.

The Third World thing quickly becomes a horror. An earth-quake in 1976 kills 25,000 Indians and flattens my lovely highland towns. Lucas Garcia turns Guatemala into a burial ground with a policy nothing short of genocide. The rooms where my boys stayed become torture chambers. Salvador erupts: an Archbishop, a Jesuit and four American religious women die from death squads. Nicaragua's promising beginning is soured, and Reagan's ideological stance pushes it into the arms of Russia. My community turns away from interest in the Third World insights I've so laboriously acquired and want so deeply to cue our lads into. That old record, who needs it? I get publicly criticized by students and faculty members and get to be known as a radical by parents; my joy at General Congregation 32, its decree on structural justice as an essential part of our apostolate, and its statements on solidarity with the poor quickly turns to dismay and frustration when for eight years in the province nothing happens. I voice concern. I ask hard questions about our work. I'm treated like a province rebel, a maverick, a peripheral voice out of step with the reigning mandarins. My local efforts in the sophomore program are finally blown apart without an in-depth evaluation. I feel increasingly that ten years of social aware-ness education and hard work are down the drain.

Age advances: teeth go, hair thins, hearing diminishes, diabetes arrives, fatigue comes faster, I drop closed retreats and CLC work and have to cut back on class. The house of my early years is almost gone now. The last and the hardest step is that in this youth culture where high value is placed on energy and pizazz, on being with it, on spirit and humor, I'm feeling increasingly over the hill. The indulgent smile, the eyes that slide over you and center on the engaging young, the comment not responded to: all make me feel like dead leaves, trampled over as of no consequence, not consulted, not valued, kept on as a favor but not as a precious asset. I feel this very deeply in day-to-day living. And so, systematically, this house is gunned down. The wreckage is complete in 1986.

Yes, I'm conscious as I experience this image of the Lord as artillery captain demolishing with glee my shiny house, that he did not do this directly. The reality of life and the unfolding of time and free choice did. Yet beyond and behind it all was this Lord at work, using my history as it unfolded, purifying me of my false selfish self in the only way that really works. This I could not do myself. My own efforts would only rivet that false self into an important self. But the Lord was doing it all the while and I finally realized it.

The next image came sudden, clear, and strong, and it filled me with wonder and joy. As I stood there looking at the ruins of my house, new walls, strong and clean, began to shoot up right before my eyes and take their position in the brand new house beginning to be built.

This time it's a completely solid house, for it's the Lord's house, not mine. It's grounded firmly in my own emptiness and poverty before the Lord, my own deep need for him and in myself as radical capacity for God.

The details of this new house fill in quickly as I walk. At the moment of my deepest need, only months after I quit as superior, the Lord was waiting for me in Rome at John's tomb. Then four years of continual and strong experience of God: the Campion Scripture class, and my first directed retreat, and the Holy Spirit night along the lake, climaxed by my first summer in Guatemala with experience of Christ's poor; the homesickness for God in a bout with depression; John of the Cross and Berkeley; and then painful years ending in 1981 with Lorraine's "John, you have an authentic call to the Person of God"; the coming of Merton into my life, "You God, you alone"; Gene Merz and his affirmation, "Sing your own song, John; no, God's song in you"; beginning to unwrap God's gift in writing my journal; Leiweke and his seal on the movements within, Finley and the awakening call: my true self at last seen as basically *capacity* for the living God, an emptiness he longs to fill, "God alone"; the cosmic dance and the storm at Notre Dame; the woman with the alabaster jar; Darlene at Easter; and now this retreat, God's presence and the surprises of the new house being constructed by the Lord, amid the ruins of the old.

Now a sudden feeling that over the years deep, decisive things have been done by the Lord and by life. The feeling that the old self, the old identity is gone almost entirely: the false self I erected, the facade boy-priest, boy-superior, renewal whiz, justice expert are gone, and gone for good. So let's let it all go gladly; let it fade into the past.

Go with the new walls rising, the new self springing up: at first fragile, tentative, wavering, but gathering strength as the years go on and the direction becomes clearer. This new house is my true self touched by God, totally God's gift, his doing and his alone.

Suddenly, I feel that all the frustration of the years has lifted. Yes, it was right for me to do all that I did, for all to happen that happened. It was the Lord's way to collapse this facade-self and to do it in a realistic way, step by step, for this was the condition for the new thing to come. The whole process took place gradually, and I'm still in one piece and none the worse for wear. Now it all makes sense.

The fine thing about this new house is that few will ever know or suspect it, for it's all God's gift and surprise. "He who is mighty has done great things for me!"

Now, at last, I feel rising in me the desire voiced in the third mode of humility in Ignatius' Spiritual Exercises. How often I've struggled with that great height; yet now it is something I feel the Lord has led me to: not just to be patient when I'm passed over by others, treated with little esteem by my confreres or as of no account, or even flat-out rejected; but to desire it, even to rejoice with it and so be more closely iden-tified with the Jesus who was passed over, not esteemed, regarded as an impractical dreamer, misunderstood, and rejected by all the big people. This quiet contentment, this gentle rejoicing in identi-fication with Jesus and more radical seeking of the Lord radiates through me now and attracts me.

I complete my walk and sunshine begins to break through the days of rain and cloud. In this short hour and a half, so much has come together; this image of the old shiny house that I built, of the Lord shooting it all apart into ruins, and of the new, clean, strong house rising up came on me so easily and naturally, growing swiftly and integrally and with such a synthe-tic sweep over my life and with such clarity of insight and nuance that I'm amazed. I'm peaceful and happy and grateful to God. I have a feeling that my life story makes sense and is whole at last, and the way now is clear to the end.

Haltingly at first and then with greater confidence and clarity, I explain to Joan what happened this Sunday morning. As I speak, she is moved; I watch tears come to her eyes as she walks with me through it; she can hardly speak. Finally she says slowly, deliberately, with understatement typical of her, "John, it's so profound, a story full of wonder. So much to have happen." Then she asks me to clarify two things. Her first question. "What kind of God is it that levels the house you had so carefully built for all these years? Is he an angry God?" My immediate response: "Oh, no! He was supremely joyful, like a happy kid with a firecracker on the Fourth of July. He was the God of the cosmic dance at play in his creation, the Risen Lord with a victorious grin celebrating a new and risen life, a final victory; the God who radiates an infectious joy that pervades me."

Her second question. "What is God saying to you about all this?" My response is immediate and intuitive and sure. "He is saying something positive. He is telling me to relax and go with the new self he's building, this new house that is totally his. 'Look I'm the Molder, the Potter. I made you as you really are, in your depths. So be the poetic, mystical, longing, affective person you are, the one who thrills to beauty, to a sense of one in all, the awe and grandeur and sublimity of all I've made and do. That's a good self, the one I made, the one I awakened at age fourteen the emptiness that cries out for my fullness, the capacity that longs for its filling. Follow my lead, trust me in the way I'm leading you, in this new birth of your new self.'" Then I stop. Joan says simply: "John, trust your God. Keep letting

him do what he wants in you. Stay with it close to your God.
Take your deep feelings always to him, express them as directly
as you can to him, talk them over with him. This is where you
will find him."

Now I know that frustration and stuckness are gone, at a
radical level, and that somehow or other I've finally broken out
into the clear. The journey stretching before me seems clear
now. I am to live the now, the moment and nothing beyond
that. There's no longer need to put two and two together, no
self-projects to construct, no need to produce results; there's
just the now, the only moment I have; so enjoy it and find the
Lord in that moment.

On Tuesday, two days later, Psalm 37 speaks directly to me
and seems to wrap up the whole experience.

> Commit to the Lord your journey. Trust in him and he
> will act. Leave it to the Lord and wait for him. Give up your
> anger and forsake your frustrations. They will only harm
> you. Instead take delight in the Lord.

You are made for God and God alone. In your depths you
are capacity for him. Journey toward the Lord these years
ahead. You already possess what you will see in face-to-face
vision some day. After some years, in full risen life, nothing will
hold you back from the vision of Father, Son, and Spirit who
will fill your finite heart to fullness. Meanwhile be the wandering comet captured in your life history by the gravity of the sun,
accelerating more and more surely, plunging into the sun to be
transformed and transfused by the living God who calls you
beloved. Yes, then you can give full reign to intensity, to the
ecstasy of your heart and exult forever in the center of the light.
Meanwhile, do what you can, but be your deepest self. Cut out
the Martha in you, so compulsive over the piddly things that
are not worth a damn, the preening of the false self, the precious
ego we make the hub of the universe and spend a whole lifetime
protecting and furthering: a useless pursuit. One thing alone,
John, is necessary.

So, let Mary grow: the self that is emptiness, that is capacity for the knowing God; the self that is awakened by God's first touch, that stands freer with each new awakening; the self that is step by step purified by God's action, that grows and develops strong under his invitation and fostering care.

All this is history of God's love working itself out in the stuff of a human life, a history that ends in endless ecstasy in the bosom of the Trinity.

> For all that has been, thanks,
> For all that will be, yes.
>
> A traveler toward the dawn,
> John Eagan, S.J.

# 15

## His Last Month—Spiritual Notes

John was told on Saturday, March 14, that he had inoperable cancer of the pancreas, metastasized in the liver.

The following jottings from his daily spiritual notes chronicle the period of pain and uncertainty up to March 14, and then after that day express his self-offering once again to the Lord and how he planned to live out his remaining time. This privileged, intimate look into John's soul reveals not only how he coped, brought loose ends together, prepared for his final journey to God, but what it's all about. They are unedited.

March 1: Two weeks of off-and-on bewildering sickness—tension and dizziness—the pain in stomach—to shoulder to under rib to throat—queasiness—to middle of back. A general nervousness. ... now at 5:00 you feel a little bad but basically free ... so relax, accept the day as it is, let the tension drop off, all there is is today—just today. God's time.

March 3: Ash Wednesday. [His doctor ordered him to the hospital for a week, then bed rest at home.] So there goes March. Give it your suscipe; purification, invitation; this one day, enjoy it and thank God.

March 13: [The morning before the CAT scan.] Some thoughts this morn:

1) O, that today you would hear my voice; harden not your heart. John—my voice calls now this way—walk this path with trust, John—take this adventure as adventure and learn from it. I beckon you, I call you. Your life and your years are in my

hands. Trust and walk on. Be open to this.

2) *Suscipe.* Take, Lord, myself—all and all—into your hands. So as little worry as possible about this CAT scan—like an x-ray only better—go into it as adventure—a 20-30 minute thing—now you'll know what people go thru ... take what you have, the present moment—this morning—this day and find the Lord in it. No need to face anything till I find out—last time nothing—so, no sweat.

March 16: [He knows he has cancer; he has decided against chemotherapy or surgery. He is back home at Marquette.] Come then, my beloved, come with me ... winter is over—the rains have stopped—out in the countryside flowers are blooming. This is the time for singing—the song of the doves is heard in our land. Come then, my beloved, come with me.

The Lord's voice—speaking to me clearly in the middle of March—come home now, John—at last to be with me forever ...

[In the chapel in the morning] As the deer thirsts for running streams so my heart thirsts for you the living God. Deep calls out to deep. In the head of the book it is written, I come to do your will, O Lord. My meat is to do the will of him who sent me.

[The notes become more fragmented, less legible.]

— my deepest self—a created capacity for God
— to take each day one by one, thank God for it. This is the day the Lord has made—let us rejoice and be glad in it.
— To simply be with this Lord who indwells in me all day long—just to be in his presence.
— Does something molded say to its molder—why did you make me like this? No! But yes to the Great Potter.
— We already possess that for which we seek.
— Yes, it all makes sense. This story is all coming to a point—sixty-one years of it to this moment, this time—this focusing on you, Lord—a sense of wholeness.
— With an everlasting love I have loved you, John ... the God who comes to fill our infinite emptiness with his infinite fullness.
— Lord, give me yourself; draw me to You.
— Come to me—if you labor and are heavily burdened and I will refresh you—give you rest. My son, give me

yourself. My heart and my flesh cry out for you, the living God. Oh, God, you are my God whom I seek; my flesh pines, my soul thirsts.

— Your way of prayer—bring everything in your life now to him—tell him about it, talk it over with him.

— I am the Good Shepherd. John, I promise you: I'll lead you out to rich pastures. Trust that Good Shepherd's leadings.

— What God wants, John, is YOU.

— You are my God—apart from you I have no good.

— Lord, which way are you going with me? Suddenly all pieces of mosaic fall into place. Now I can see the whole story.

— ... a real gift—warning—definite time frame, chance to pull things together.

— walk with dogged fidelity all the way to the end.

— Psalm 38. How frail I am, my life as nought before you, only a breath, like a vapor our restless pursuits, for what do I wait now, O Lord, for you, I am just a wayfarer, a traveler towards the dawn.

March 22: [He wrote his friends at St. John Neumann, the parish where he had said two Masses and preached every Sunday for four years.]

A final word. I do want to give each of you my warm thanks for continually over the years welcoming me to St. John's as your priest. You came into my life when I was searching for more adult ministry. And I really look upon you as God's answer to my search: God's wonderful people, welcoming, encouraging, appreciative, open and flexible, giving me over and over again the gift of your friendship. You should know— it is a privilege for me to have served you these years—breaking open the Word of the Lord, sharing the great Eucharistic Sacrifice with you, and then bringing you Jesus Christ in Communion. So many of these have been blessed experiences of God's closeness for me and so rich grace in my life. Finally— you have something great going at St. John Neumann—may it grow and grow.

In the Lord,
Fr. John Eagan, S.J.

March 24: The great image
  the journey home into the heart of God
  the journey into the inner life of the Trinity
  the journey to ecstatic Beatifying Vision
  we are made for ecstasy, nothing less
  each moment of closeness to God, only
        a preview of what's ahead
        Total intimacy—we shall see him as he is
        Total love —with your whole heart's intensity
        Total joy —cascading all over you
        And this forever ...
        a few months——and then
  the traveler toward the dawn
        dawn breaking love as I travel
  the wandering comet finally captured by the gravity of
        the sun—plunging into its fiery depths—to full
        union ...
  so many life-journeys—to San Diego—to Rainier—to
        Yosemite—to Glacier—to Rome and Florence—to
        Canada—such looking forward to—such joy
  now, this final, last journey—the best of them all—
        and the last
  Admittedly a sense of relief, a sense of freedom,
        freedom from deadline—a clean, clear closure
  Yes, at age sixty-one, I've seen much of what I wanted to,
        done much of what I've wanted to really ...
        look at world on evening TV, newspapers, problems
        proliferating
        I've had enough of it—a wanting to go home to God
        I'm homesick—and you've created a lot of that by
            religious experience and desire on retreats, Lord,
            a far, far better life ahead
        I feel few attachments left
        Rather a desire to go home to you
            You God, you—says it all
            You God, you .....
  The fitness of time—it's just the right time to wind
  up and go
        if I could choose, this would be the time to

choose ... really ...
To live in the present moment
    and to say yes to your loving God at every step of
    the way ...

The way I want to handle all this:
    1. Center on others, their interests, how they are doing
       *warmth & encouragement* on their world
       vs. long, long recitals of my medical story
    2. Keep in touch with the living
    3. when talk about self and your condition
       humor
       the positive—I taught today
       what I'm trying to do—positively
                  theologically
       what I'm going toward
    4. above all,
       center not on present pain
       but on whole process
       journey into God
       risen life
       exploration of Triune God
       good I can do
       just a little while and then glory
    5. the present moment — it's usually OK

March 30:
    The image from the owl. The swimmer: mark the salmon—coming up from the ocean—thru the river—up to the quiet hole—to spawn and then turn over—and so new life cycle. The swimmer, the climax of his adventuresome life—to the end for which he had been made.
    Walk straight on, my Son.
    Do not look back.
    Do not turn your head.
    You are going to the land of our Lord.

    Thursday, April 9: He received the green light from his doctor to go to San Francisco on April 15 to see his Jesuit brother, Joe, who was to drive him to see his beloved Yosemite Valley and its waterfalls for one last time.

Friday, April 10: He taught class for the last time.

With great effort, he had been teaching one class a day during the previous several weeks.

Sunday, April 12: The journey ends.

# 16

## Farewell

John Eagan's wake and Mass of Christian Burial were held in the spacious Jesuit Church of the Gesu at Marquette University on April 15, 1987.

A steady stream of people, beginning at 2:00 P.M., filed past the casket: present and past students, their parents, parishioners from St. John Neumann's parish, Marquette High faculty. Past students somehow spread the word so that many flew in from the East Coast and Midwest cities. On a table next to the casket were symbols of the kind of man John was: his skis and hiking boots, pictures of his ordination and ministry, an album of photos he had taken of the mountains and lakes he loved, photos of students on hiking and camping trips, Marquette High yearbook pictures, and a copy of the early pages of his journal, which a mother of one of his former students had finished typing just three days before.

The Mass at 5:30 was a joyful event concelebrated by sixty-five priests and attended by over 1,000 people, with the overflow in the aisles and into the vestibule. A choir of young Jesuit priests sang. Fr. Jeff Loebl, whom John had taught and counseled as a Marquette High student and who was now a young Jesuit priest in the Marquette High preached the homily. After the Mass the casket was reopened for forty-five minutes to give all in the large crowd a chance to pay their final respects.

How does one pay tribute to an "ordinary" priest who, as a high school teacher, was able to influence lives so widely and so deeply? How does one capture a soul nourished so richly in secret by the Lord who destroys and rebuilds houses? There were so many attempts to convey John's contagious aliveness, written both during and after his life here, that it would take another small volume to contain them. Let one, then, stand for all: a poem written by one of John's former students, Jim Wilkinson.

### John Eagan - Final Thoughts?

I've got so few words left—

What do I want to say?


Wait.

I hear music,

And it's getting closer.

Ha! It's Mahler.

I always knew it—

Classical music

Is celestial music.


God, I'm so tired.

I pushed this body,

Maybe further than it ought to go.

Don't get me wrong—

No regrets.

These legs

Climbed mountains in Guatemala

And swam cold Lake Superior.

Oh, my. What a time.

Yes, I caught more than one

Sunrise in Yosemite,

And bathed in many a waterfall.

Remember the glorious sun and powder

Of Aspen,

And the hikes to the peaks in Glacier Park?

Ah!

I'm going to miss those things.

I'm so tired.

Am I making any sense?

My feet don't even touch the ground anymore.

I've been on my way

For a long time now.

No regrets.

I can't believe what I'm seeing.

Are angels really

Riding bikes these days?

Oh, my.

I know what you're here for,

And I have to admit,

I'm ready.

It's getting awful tough

To carry even these thin bones.

I hope you don't mind

If I hop on the back of your bike.

I'd like to say a few more goodbyes,

But, hey,

When it's time,

It's time.

I'll tell, you, angel,

That body wasn't serving me too well

Near the end,

But I was still pretty fond of it,

Considering it was the only one I had.


I'm free, now, aren't I?

Then I'm sure God wouldn't mind

If, on our way back home,

We took one quick swing

Over the Grand Tetons and Yosemite.